"In clear and accessible prose, Paul Louis Metzger walks us through Jesus' simple but revolutionary introduction to the upside-down kingdom of God . . . With the heart of a friend and the mind of a scholar, Metzger guides us through the cultural setting and contemporary relevance for each of Jesus' beatitudes. This highly readable book provides a winsome vision for any Christian hungering to walk afresh in the way of Jesus. But it's also an exceptional resource for preachers and teachers who want to lead their people through this potent and beautiful section of Scripture."

—Matt Woodley
Editor of *Preaching Today*, Author of *The Gospel of Matthew: God with Us*

"*Beatitudes, Not Platitudes* is one of the few books in recent memory that meets more than one need in the church today. It is theologically informative and devotionally inspirational, while at the same time, it encourages us to be more sensitive to the social challenges that many are struggling to overcome. Paul Louis Metzger has written a masterpiece for our times."

—Jimi Calhoun
Lead Pastor, Bridging Austin, Author of *A Story of Rhythm and Grace: What the Church Can Learn from Rock and Roll About Healing the Racial Divide*

"The Beatitudes are spiritual treasures. They are like diamonds that never lose their value or beauty with the passing of time. However, too often our church theologies and cultural challenges gloss them over with a thick veneer that hides their true meaning. In *Beatitudes, Not Platitudes*, Paul Louis Metzger skillfully wipes off the dust, helping the reader rediscover the true light, color and symmetry of these great diamonds. Metzger's style is clear, direct, biblical, and well-illustrated."

—Alex Awad

Retired Pastor of East Jerusalem Baptist Church, Author of *Palestinian Memories: The Story of a Palestinian Mother and Her People*

"What philosophers across the ages have described as 'the good life' Jesus redefines as 'the blessed life,' but not without some surprising promises. In the lucid and devotional prose of Paul Louis Metzger, the Beatitudes of Jesus are no mere platitudes. They challenge conventional notions of success and popularity, revealing the paradoxes of the upside-down kingdom. This book is a must-read—chock full of life-transforming and world-changing possibilities."

—Paul N. Anderson

Professor of Biblical and Quaker Studies, George Fox University, Author of *From Crisis to Christ: A Contextual Introduction to the New Testament, Following Jesus: The Heart of Faith and Practice*

BEATITUDES, NOT PLATITUDES

BEATITUDES, NOT PLATITUDES

Jesus' Invitation to the Good Life

Paul Louis Metzger

CASCADE *Books* • Eugene, Oregon

BEATITUDES, NOT PLATITUDES
Jesus' Invitation to the Good Life

Cascacde Books
An Imprint of Wipf and Stock Publishers
199 W. 8th Ave., Suite 3
Eugene, OR 97401

www.wipfandstock.com

PAPERBACK ISBN: 978-1-5326-3313-3
HARDCOVER ISBN: 978-1-5326-3315-7
EBOOK ISBN: 978-1-5326-3314-0

Cataloguing-in-Publication data:

Names: Metzger, Paul Louis
Title: Beatitudes, not platitudes : Jesus' invitation to the good life / Paul Louis
    Metzger.
Description: Eugene, OR: Cascade Books, 2018 | Includes bibliographical refer-
    ences and index.
Identifiers: ISBN 978-1-5326-3313-3 (paperback) | ISBN 978-1-5326-3315-7
    (hardcover) | ISBN 978-1-5326-3314-0 (ebook)
Subjects: LCSH: Beatitudes | Sermon on the mount | Bible. Matthew—Criticism,
    interpretation, etc. | Discipling (Christianity)
Classification: BT380 M345 2018 (paperback) | BT380 (ebook)

Manufactured in the U.S.A.   03/20/18

*To my Cross-Cultural Engagement cohort
for their long-suffering love on display with me.*

*To the persecuted church across the globe
for suffering long with Jesus.*

Contents

Acknowledgments

The Reformation teaching *Sola Scriptura* was never intended to promote a solitary-confinement approach to reading Scripture and living out the Christian life. And yet, one might be led to think in our individualistic, "self-made-man" context that spiritual formation is all about "I did it my way." However, when one comes to terms with the Beatitudes and Sermon on the Mount, the most honest-hearted and realistic in our midst soon realize we can't get very far on our own. We need the courage and encouragement of Jesus and his community as they envision and embody these spiritual values for and with us.

The same point applies to anyone writing a book on the Beatitudes or Sermon on the Mount. No one can write about it alone. With this point in mind, I wish to acknowledge those who have collaborated with me in one way or another in this spiritual exercise.

For starters, those who helped me finish up the volume—Sara Mannen and Derrick Peterson—deserve special mention. There are many reasons why there is only one Rabbi in the Christian life—Jesus. The rest of us are students. These two students of mine have been relational, intellectual, and spiritual gifts as dialogue partners and colleagues. While theirs is the kingdom of heaven (present tense), their ultimate reward is in heaven, when they will receive "total consciousness," to allude to an extrabiblical though authoritative line from Bill Murray in *Caddyshack*!

Acknowledgments

Robin Parry of Cascade/Wipf & Stock provided invaluable encouragement and input, as did others at the publishing house. Two of the qualities I most admire of my publisher are: first, their commitment to the printed word and Christian scholarship that goes far beyond market demands; and second, their intentionality in being more than a publishing house that issues Christian books to one that is truly a Christian community. While they might desire a more immediate reward, they will likely have to wait on the reception of this book, as the divine jury is still out with me!

No book I write can see the light of day without paying tribute to my wife Mariko and children Christopher and Julianne, who have learned well the meaning of mourning my spiritual state. My new daughter-in-law Keyonna and granddaughter Jaylah will learn well its meaning, too! I am very grateful to the Lord for being so blessed by all of them.

Lastly, I wish to pay tribute to my Doctor of Ministry and Master of Arts in Applied Theology cohort in Cross-Cultural Engagement for New Wine, New Wineskins at Multnomah Biblical Seminary/Multnomah University. Their engagement of preliminary lectures and my Patheos blog posts at Uncommon God, Common Good on the Beatitudes for a course on Jesus' countercultural kingdom was stimulating, sharpening, and life-giving. These colleagues comprehend G. K. Chesterton's words that the Christian faith has not been tried and found wanting, but found difficult and left untried. So, they've been busy trying on Jesus' Beatitudes for size. In addition to cohort collaboration in class, their personal stories and the stories of other friends accounted for in the cultural reflection pieces (sometimes with names changed) helped the biblical meditations set forth in this volume take on flesh and blood. Together with the persecuted church across the globe, which shares in Jesus' struggle, I dedicate this book to them. Leadership from below and from the margins of society will increasingly mark the church's life in the States in the years ahead, just like in other countries. I have so much to learn from these brothers and sisters in other lands as they lay down their lives for Jesus, captured by his undying love.

Introduction

The Beatitudes Are Not Dead Metaphors
or Well-Worn, Outgrown Platitudes.
Dare Try Them On for Size.

The first time I recall hearing a sermon series on the Beatitudes and Sermon on the Mount was at a church in 1999. The pastor was relatively new to the large congregation (and so were we). And so, he might not have picked up that this was the first time many of them had heard a series on Matthew 5–7. One Sunday morning, I distinctively heard a puzzled parishioner say to a spouse, "Why is he preaching on the Sermon on the Mount? It has nothing to do with the church. It's addressed to Israel." Regardless of the brand of dispensational theology espoused by this parishioner, I wish the congregation had sensed that the beatitude of mercy had something to do with them, as they sent the pastor packing not long afterward (supposedly due to his approach to biblical exposition). Surely, Jesus' longest recorded sermon has something to say to the church on mercy, meekness, and a great deal more! Moreover, given that Jesus instructs his followers in the Great Commission to teach new disciples to obey *everything* Jesus has taught and commanded them (Matt 28:18–20), this would certainly include the instructions recorded in the Sermon on the Mount. Wherever the Great Commission goes, so too goes the Sermon on the Mount.

Far from being overused, no longer interesting and meaningful, the Beatitudes are underused. They are not Nietzschean dead metaphors or well-worn, outgrown ethical platitudes. Often, the Beatitudes are not accounted for and applied because they are found to be all-too striking, mind-blowing, and hard. It reminds me of G. K. Chesterton's claim: "The Christian ideal has not been tried and found wanting. It has been found difficult; and left untried."[1] If only we would dare try them on for size![2]

I have found increasingly that the Beatitudes and the Sermon on the Mount have pressing importance for the church in North America.[3] No matter what brand of theology or denomination, we can all benefit from the Lord's address to his disciples—an exodus community on its way through the wilderness to the promised land. As the church finds itself increasingly displaced from the broader culture, not unlike Israel and the church in Jesus' day, perhaps it will see it was enslaved in Egypt or in exile under the rule of Assyria, Babylon, or Rome for a very long time and that it needs to reconfigure its spiritual imagination and practices in view of Jesus' messianic law. Just as the Romans sacked Jerusalem and destroyed the temple, leading to the rebuilding of the Jewish faith on different spiritual soil, so the church in America can no longer pursue allegiance with America (the new Rome?). While the church-state alliance may come to an end more by erosion than eradication, Christendom is waning. Matthew's Gospel with its employment of the Beatitudes and Sermon on the Mount may very well have been written against the backdrop of the destruction of the temple.

---

1. Chesterton, *What's Wrong with the World*, 37.

2. The Beatitudes, like the Sermon on the Mount as a whole, provide a profound, radical, and imposing vision of what Jesus' kingdom entails. Faced with this reality, many have sought to domesticate its message: "The history of the impact of the Sermon on the Mount can largely be described in terms of an attempt to domesticate everything in it that is shocking, demanding, and uncompromising, and render it harmless. 'Time and time again,' writes Gunther Bornkamm, 'Christianity, especially with the assistance of its theology, has known so well and still knows how to intercept, so to speak, the thrust of Jesus' challenge, to divert it and to settle down peacefully in spite of it.'" Lapide, *The Sermon on the Mount*, 3.

3. Frederick Bruner's *Matthew: A Commentary* and Matt Woodley's *The Gospel of Matthew* are good sources for those looking for writers who engage and exegete the biblical text and move to the contemporary cultural context.

Whether prior to or after the temple's destruction, it can and must serve as a beneficial resource for reframing the faith in a post-Christendom context[4] if we are to embrace and embody the good life that Jesus envisions.[5]

Jesus' counter-cultural community and shalom of a peaceful and just rule stood in stark contrast to the *Pax Romana* (Peace of Rome) with its retributive system.[6] Moreover, he identified with the common people in a radically different manner than the shepherds of Israel did—or rather, did not do: the people he served were sheep without shepherds (Matt 9:36; compare Matt 4:23 with 9:35). According to Jürgen Moltmann, Bismarck claimed that no country could be ruled by the Sermon on the Mount, and instead offered Germany "blood and iron." (More recently, Texas megachurch pastor Robert Jeffress claimed, while asserting that President Trump has the authority to take out Kim Jong Un in North Korea: "A Christian writer asked me, 'Don't you want the president

---

4. I refer to post-Christendom over against post-Christian in that Christianity is still the dominant religion in the United States, with the majority (however slight) of the population identifying with the Christian faith in some manner. While Christian privileges are increasingly waning, the church has not undergone widespread persecution as a religious minority in the States.

5. Most scholars believe Matthew was written around AD 85, though some argue for a much earlier origination. For the latter, see for example Hendriksen, *The Gospel of Matthew*, 92–97; Gundry, *Matthew*, 599–609. Gundry believes Matthew was written no later than AD 63. W. D. Davies maintains that Matthew's Gospel was written sometime after AD 70 (the year of the destruction of the temple in Jerusalem), and in response to the rebuilding of rabbinic Judaism in Jamnia. Jesus' teaching in the Sermon on the Mount (I maintain that Jesus' address was most likely delivered on a mountain near the Sea of Galilee in Northern Israel) is presented as the new *Halakhah*, or messianic law. See Davies, *The Setting of the Sermon on the Mount*, 88. Just as Jesus is presented as the messianic fulfillment of the Davidic kingship in Matthew's genealogy, so this sermon on a mountain may function to present Jesus as the new Moses to Jewish people and gentile adherents of Judaism. However, doubt has been cast on whether the placement of five major teaching sections (beginning with the Sermon on the Mount) following narrative sections respectively functions to present Jesus' law as the fulfillment of the Mosaic law. In addition to Davies on this subject (91–126), see for example France, *The Gospel of Matthew*, 2–3.

6. Consider Moltmann, *The Crucified God*, 136–45, for his analysis of Jesus' confrontation of the Roman system of retribution.

to embody the Sermon on the Mount?' . . . I said absolutely not"[7]). Whether or not a country can be governed according to the Beatitudes, the church must be. So, as Moltmann claims, the point is not to politicize churches, but to Christianize churches and Christians' political existence in view of the Sermon on the Mount.[8]

The Sermon on the Mount is not an apolitical treatise, but one that is very political.[9] It presents Jesus' eschatological kingdom vision for his people on their way from Egypt to the promised land in the here and now. As such, the Beatitudes find their home in the Jewish scriptural tradition. One finds beatitudes in various Old Testament texts. Consider such verses as Psalm 1:1, 2:12, Proverbs 8:34, Isaiah 56:2, and Daniel 12:12. One also finds blessings set forth in contrast to curses, as in Genesis 27 and Deuteronomy 27–28. Jesus may have originally delivered the Beatitudes along with curses, as one finds recorded in Luke 6:20–26. Consider, too, that there are curses set forth in Matthew 23:13–29.[10] In fact, it could be the case that the curses set forth in Matthew 23:13–29 are intended to function as the literary equivalent to the Beatitudes in Matthew 5, forming an *inclusio* or literary envelope for Jesus' public ministry.[11] The blessings take place in Jesus' first recorded public sermon and the curses take place in his last recorded public sermon in Matthew's Gospel. Against the backdrop of Moses, Israel, and the law (Deut 27–28), God honors and blesses those whose identity, allegiance, and activity are aligned with Jesus' life and law, and reproaches those whose lives oppose Jesus and his

---

7. Bailey, "'God Has Given Trump Authority to Take Out Kim Jong Un,' Evangelical Adviser Says," August 8, 2017.

8. Moltmann, *God for a Secular Society*, 49.

9. See Blomberg's discussion of various views on Jesus as a social reformer in his work, *Jesus and the Gospels*, 212–14. Consider also Greenman, Larsen, and Spencer, eds., *The Sermon on the Mount through the Centuries*.

10. Keener, *The Gospel of Matthew*, 165.

11. See N. T. Wright's discussion of the Beatitudes and curses in Matthew 5 and 23 respectively and his linking of them to the blessings and curses in Deuteronomy 27 and 28 in *The New Testament and the People of God*, 386–88. See also the comparisons and contrasts of the blessings and curses in Matthew 5 and Matthew 23 in Hanson's article, "How Honorable! How Shameful!" 101–4.

word. In the conclusion, we will come full circle to this place where we have begun (like a literary envelope) where the blessings and curses set forth in Matthew 5 and Matthew 23 respectively will be presented in liturgical form in a manner equivalent to the declarations of blessings and curses from Mount Gerizim and Mount Ebal in Deuteronomy 27:11–14.

The present volume is a devotional and spiritual-formation book that involves biblical meditations along with contemporary cultural commentary and questions for small-group engagement. Some devotional books can give you the sense that grace is not only free, but it is "cheap," as Dietrich Bonhoeffer lamented about the state of grace in his day, having no bearing on anyone or anything around you. All that matters are pious sentiments. Bonhoeffer writes in his book on discipleship in which he expounds upon the Sermon on the Mount, "Cheap grace is the grace we bestow on ourselves. Cheap grace is the preaching of forgiveness without requiring repentance, baptism without church discipline, Communion without confession. . . . Cheap grace is grace without discipleship, grace without the cross, grace without Jesus Christ, living and incarnate."[12] This is a far-cry from what Matthew's presentation of Jesus' sermon envisions. As Craig Keener notes, "The beatitudes indicate that one who truly repents in light of the coming kingdom will treat one's neighbors rightly. No one who has humbled himself or herself before God, depending on the just judge to vindicate them in his coming day of judgment, can act with wanton self-interest in relationships."[13] Personal relationship with Jesus, as often heard in Christian circles, can never entail an individual in isolation who apart from a warm feeling toward the Lord (disconnected from consideration of his incarnate reality) promotes indifference toward others. By no means does Jesus offer us "a private spirituality in the present and a 'heavenly salvation' in the future."[14] Rather, just as Jesus proclaimed the Beatitudes and

---

12. Bonhoeffer, *The Cost of Discipleship*, 44–45.

13. Keener, *The Gospel of Matthew*, 165.

14. See Wright's critique of this privatized, other-worldly orientation in *The Challenge of Jesus*, 7. It is also important to note that the Sermon on the

Sermon on the Mount in public to his disciples with the crowds assembled, so he intends for his disciples to embody his message of the inbreaking of the eschatological kingdom in his person publicly to the world.

While devotional books can foster an individualism that does not account for Christian discipleship, spiritual-formation books for Christian discipleship can have the appearance of being religious self-help manuals that teach one to follow Jesus in one's own strength. Nothing could be further from the truth when it comes to the Sermon on the Mount. Jesus does not expect us to pick ourselves up by the bootstraps and do religion by our lonesome. From Matthew 1:23 to the very last verse—Matthew 28:20, Matthew emphasizes that we are not alone. God in Jesus is with us—Immanuel.

Matthew 28:20 is the close of the Great Commission. The Great Commission is the Great Communion in which we participate in the life of the triune God while bearing witness to the good news of God calling all humanity to respond to his personal love through faith in Jesus every day of the year across the globe. In Matthew 28:18–20, we find that we are called to baptize people into the name of the Father, Son, and Spirit, teaching Jesus' disciples to obey his commandments which are summed up in loving God with all our hearts and our neighbors as ourselves (Matt 22:34–40). As Jesus goes with us, and the Spirit dwells in us and empowers us,[15] we invite people to enter God's community as

---

Mount and the Beatitudes do not provide us with the roadmap for personal salvation. Rather, they present us with Jesus first and foremost. As Scot McKnight writes, "The gospel is a message about Jesus first and foremost and not first a message about us and our salvation. The King saves, but the gospel is news about the arrival of the King." The Sermon on the Mount is gospel. As McKnight writes, "If the gospel is a declaration of who Jesus is, the Sermon on the Mount, in context, is gospel. The recorded response to the Sermon is the intended response for all of us, and that question—Who does he think he is?!—is the fundamental gospel question to answer." McKnight, "The Sermon on the Mount as Gospel." See also McKnight, *The King Jesus Gospel*, 92–113.

15. The same Spirit through whom Jesus was conceived (Matt 1:18), who descended on him in the event of his baptism (Matt 3:16), who rests upon him as he proclaims justice to the gentiles (Matt 12:18), with whom Jesus baptizes his followers (Matt 3:11), who led him into the wilderness to be tempted by

members of the divine family. D. A. Carson asserts that Matthew ends with "promise" rather than "commission" in Matthew 28:20: "Our English 'always' masks a Greek expression found only here, and meaning 'the whole of every day.' Jesus promises to be with His disciples, as they make disciples of others, not only on the long haul, 'but the whole of every day,' 'to the very end of the age.'"[16]

Just as Jesus sends the church into the world with the promise of his presence, so, too, he sends us in community. With this point in mind, Jesus addresses the Sermon on the Mount to his church, not solitary individuals. All the beatitudes, for example, are addressed to a plural referent. We are not intended to live the Beatitude reality alone, but in the presence of Jesus and fellow disciples. Since this is the case, it is best to engage this book on the Beatitudes in the context of community rather than in an isolated manner. Truly, those who are poor in spirit (Matt 5:3) will realize that they cannot go it alone. The poor (plural) in spirit are blessed and honored. Theirs is the kingdom of heaven. They are also those (plural) who are persecuted because of righteousness (Matt 5:10). Following verse 10, Jesus moves from the third person plural to the second person plural and says that while the world ridicules and shames you (plural), you (plural) are to rejoice and exult, for your honorable reward in the kingdom of heaven (to which you belong) is great. Not only do you suffer with Jesus, but also with the prophets of old who came before you, and who were persecuted in the same manner. Jesus' first disciples were not alone, but operated as a community. Thus, we should as well. There is strength and resilience in numbers.

Just as Jesus does not expect us to go it alone, he does not expect that we can make the Beatitudes operative in our lives. Again, those who are poor in spirit and who mourn their spiritual state realize they are in need of their Lord at every turn. What Karl Barth said of the kingdom of God in reflecting on the closing lines

---

the devil (Matt 4:1), and through whom Jesus casts out demons (Matt 12:28) endows his followers with his presence, guiding and illumining them (Matt 10:20).

16. D. A. Carson, *God with Us*, 163.

of the Rule of Benedict applies here as well. It is not, as Benedict suggested, by doing these things (the disciplines, virtues, or habits Benedict articulated) that the eschatological kingdom of God breaks into our midst, but by the Lord of the kingdom entering our midst that we do these things.[17] Certainly, we are to be meek and merciful, but these values only become embodied in our lives in vital relation to Jesus and through his call on our lives.

I have taught on the Beatitudes and Sermon on the Mount in various contexts for years and have sought to live the message out in community. Most recently, I have developed an entire Doctor of Ministry class dedicated to the Beatitudes. My Cross-Cultural Engagement cohort at Multnomah University and Seminary invests considerable thought and energy in taking to heart Jesus' teaching in Matthew 5. It is all part of our ambition to be ambassadors for Jesus' upside-down kingdom wherever we are in this world. I am dedicating this book to the cohort, and in view of the very last beatitude, to the persecuted church across the globe.

Welcome to Jesus' upside-down kingdom in which the poor in spirit are blessed and honored, as are those who mourn their spiritual state, who operate from the vantage point of meekness, who hunger and thirst for righteousness, who are merciful, who are pure in heart, who are peacemakers. No wonder, those who follow Jesus' way are persecuted and shamed by the surrounding culture, which operates downside up! With this point in mind, I hope you get comfortable reading while standing on your head. We will certainly need to become more agile in our imaginations if we wish to come to terms with Jesus' invitation to the good life as he defines and designs it. The kingdom of heaven belongs to those aligned with him.

17. Barth, *CD* IV/2, 18.

1

Blessed Are the Happy in Jesus, Not Tortured, Cheated, or Diseased Souls

Biblical Meditation

The crowds, including the disciples, were looking for happiness. However, things hadn't turned out well for many of them. Many were living a country and western song—looking for happiness in all the wrong places. They were downtrodden, bewildered, and oppressed. However, they sensed with Jesus that perhaps their fortunes were about to change. Just maybe he was the long-expected Messiah, who would liberate them from their enemies and free them from their fears. And so, they followed him, hanging on his every word, hoping that they would find happiness in him (Matt 4:23—5:2; cf. Matt 9:35–38). What about us?

All of us want to be happy, but we look for happiness in different places and with mixed results. Some of us grieve over not obtaining happiness. We are tortured souls. Others of us think we have achieved it, but we are deceived. We are cheated souls. Others of us have the proper object of happiness, but we fail to realize it. We are diseased souls. It is important that we pursue the ultimate

Good, who alone is the basis for true and lasting happiness. Our hearts will forever remain restless until they find their rest in the Good, that is, God, as St. Augustine wrote.[1] Augustine also spoke about happiness along these lines:

> How then, according to reason, ought man to live? We all certainly desire to live happily; and there is no human being but assents to this statement almost before it is made. But the title happy cannot, in my opinion, belong either to him who has not what he loves, whatever it may be, or to him who has what he loves if it is hurtful or to him who does not love what he has, although it is good in perfection. For one who seeks what he cannot obtain suffers *torture*, and one who has got what is not desirable is *cheated*, and one who does not seek for what is worth seeking for is *diseased*. Now in all these cases the mind cannot but be unhappy, and happiness and unhappiness cannot reside at the same time in one man; so in none of these cases can the man be happy. I find, then, a fourth case, where the happy life exists,—when that which is man's chief good is both loved and possessed. For what do we call enjoyment but having at hand the objects of love? And no one can be happy who does not enjoy what is man's chief good, nor is there any one who enjoys this who is not happy. We must then have at hand our chief good, if we think of living happily (emphasis added).[2]

Tortured souls observe happiness, but cannot gain it. *Cheated* souls believe they have happiness, but are deceived. *Diseased* souls have something that *should* lead to happiness, but they do not know it. Can you relate to any or all of these descriptions?

Ultimately, for Augustine, the happy or blessed life is bound up with following God—the Supreme Good—and holding to his teaching, which culminates in the revelation of Jesus Christ who unites the Old and New Testaments.[3] Or as the old song goes, there is no other way to be happy in Jesus than to trust and obey.

1. Augustine, *The Confession of St. Augustine*, I/1, 17.
2. Augustine, *Of the Morals of the Catholic Church*, III/4.
3. Ibid., VI–XI.

The conclusion to the Sermon on the Mount says as much (Matt 7:24–27). After all, who among those who build their houses on sand and watch them swept away by floodwaters are happy? The wise person who builds his or her life on Jesus' word will be happy when that house (i.e., life) remains standing.

> Everyone then who hears these words of mine and does them will be like a wise man who built his house on the rock. And the rain fell, and the floods came, and the winds blew and beat on that house, but it did not fall, because it had been founded on the rock. And everyone who hears these words of mine and does not do them will be like a foolish man who built his house on the sand. And the rain fell, and the floods came, and the winds blew and beat against that house, and it fell, and great was the fall of it. (Matt 7:24–27)

The Sermon on the Mount's closing grounds the life of wisdom and happiness in holding firmly to Jesus' teaching. Now what about the beginning of it? Jesus begins the Sermon on the Mount with eight beatitudes (Matt 5:3–10).[4] What are the Beatitudes? They are kingdom blessings (*beatitudines, benedictiones*), which indelibly mark the lives of Jesus' followers. As such, the Beatitudes or blessings do not refer to a "feel good" sentiment, that is, some ephemeral emotional state involving "warm fuzzies."[5] Rather, they reveal an objective, good standing or honorable position in God's kingdom community.[6] Indeed, while the world might shame them

4. While some scholars speak of nine beatitudes, I maintain that there are eight. Thus, I do not see the "Blessed" of verse 11 introducing a separate beatitude, but rather, expanding on the "Blessed" of verse 10. I also believe verses 3 through 10 function as a unit (with verses 11–13 unpacking further verse 10). Verses 3 and 10 serve to bring together the entire unit as a literary envelope or *inclusio*. Verses 3 and 10 end with "for theirs is the kingdom of heaven."

5. For Augustine, happiness is grounded in the being of God who is love with whom one is united, not some subjective emotional state that ebbs and flows.

6. According to Kenneth E. Bailey, "*Makarios* affirms a quality of spirituality that is already present. . . . Put in concrete terms, we could say, 'Bless-ed is the happy daughter of Mr. Jones because she will inherit the Jones's farm.' The woman in question is already the happy daughter of Mr. Jones. She's not

for being poor in spirit, for mourning their spiritual state, for meekness, for hungering and thirsting for righteousness, for being merciful, for being pure of heart, for being peacemakers, and even persecute them for their allegiance to Jesus, they are esteemed with great honor in Jesus' counter-cultural or upside-down kingdom. Those who are happy or blessed are really those who are honorable. "How honorable" are the poor in spirit, . . . who are persecuted for righteousness sake, for theirs is the kingdom of God.[7] It will be well with them.[8]

---

working to inherit the farm. Everyone knows that a key element in her happy and secure life is that she and the community around her know that the farm will one day be hers. The first statement affirms a happy state that already exists. The second statement affirms a future that allows her even now to live a happy life." Bailey, *Jesus through Middle Eastern Eyes*, 68.

7. The blessings or affirmations of honor in the Sermon on the Mount are not to be confused with the Instagram hashtag #blessed. As my colleague Sara Mannen has noted, in our current pop culture, when pictures or posts on social media are tagged with the hashtag blessed, they are usually associated with some sort of physical/material blessing or, for those who are more "spiritual," they are usually connected to model families or meaningful devotions, and the like. K. C. Hanson has argued for interpreting the makarisms (beatitudes) as "expressions of honor," and that Matthew 5:3–12 must be conceived "as a programmatic value statement: the conditions and behaviors which the community regards as honorable . . . ." Thus, one would translate them as "How honorable . . . ." See Hanson, "How Honorable! How Shameful!" 100–101; see also page 81. Hanson also writes on page 89: "But if *ashrei* and *makarios* do not refer to a ritual blessing, neither do they mean 'happy.' They are not expressions of positive human emotion. One does not feel good who fears Yahweh (Ps 112:1), or walks in Yahweh's law (Ps 119:1), or is reproved and chastened by Yahweh (Job 5:17)! Similarly, one does not feel good who mourns or is persecuted (Matt 5:4, 10). So 'happy' is a profoundly misleading translation and interpretation of the makarism (contra Moulton and Milligan: 386, and Louw and Nida 1:302). Even the idea of 'imputation of happiness' by others is misleading (contra Janzen 1965:226)." Italicized Hebrew and Greek terms in the quote have been transliterated from the original source.

8. Craig S. Keener has also weighed in on the translation of *makarioi* (plural for *makarios*): "It will be well with" may be a better translation than "blessed" or "happy" for *makarios*. See *The Gospel of Matthew*, 165–66. For the purposes of this lay-level volume, I will continue to use the far more commonly known translation of "Blessed" as it is part of the received history of translation and more familiar to lay readers. Even so, my particular exposition of the beatitudes cautions against a "feel good" happy state and resonates with

Why is this address titled the "Sermon on the Mount"? It is because Jesus went up on a mount (or mountainous place) to teach his disciples and accompanying masses about the blessed life (Matt 5:1–2).[9] While debated, it has been argued that the author is doing more than referencing the location of Jesus' address; the claim is made that the mount has symbolic and theological significance.[10] Some scholars claim that Matthew presents Jesus as a new Moses.[11] The connection has also been made between the eight Beatitudes and the Decalogue or Ten Commandments. Just as adherence to the Decalogue (Ten Commandments) was essential to experiencing God's shalom, so Jesus' Beatitudes are essential to experiencing his kingdom peace. As with the Ten Commandments in relation to the Torah (five books of Moses), the Beatitudes present the heart of Jesus' teaching recorded in the Sermon on the Mount and in Matthew's Gospel.[12] Jesus instructs us concerning what life in his kingdom entails.

the idea that the disciples who embody these qualities are "honorable" (Hanson) and that "it will be well with" them (Keener).

9. Luke's Gospel includes a parallel account often titled the Sermon on the Plain (Luke 6). An abbreviated version of the Beatitudes is found in Luke 6:20–23, and is accompanied by four curses in Luke 6:24–26.

10. See footnote 11 below.

11. See for example Robert Gundry's exposition of Matthew 5:1–10 in his *Commentary on the New Testament*, 15–16. Along this line of thinking, one might wonder if Matthew alludes to Moses going up on the mount to get God's law (Exod 24:12–18), whereas Jesus goes up the mount to give his law, which is the fulfillment of the Mosaic law. As great as Moses was, Jesus is far greater. In the history of the church, exegetes and theologians have sometimes made the connection between the second person of the Trinity (Jesus) and the Angel of the Lord to whom God alludes in Exodus 23:20–22 (which Moses and the people are to obey), as well as Jesus and the prophet like Moses, to whom Moses refers in Deuteronomy 18:15. Regarding the former, see for example Charles Ellicott's exposition of Exodus 23:20, *Ellicott's Bible Commentary*, 119–20.

12. Matthew's Gospel makes various connections between the Torah and Old Testament as a whole and Jesus' life and teaching. The genealogy of Jesus shows that he is the descendent of Abraham. It has also been argued that the genealogy presents Jesus as the fulfillment of the messianic promises bound up with the royal line of King David and agent of God's blessings to the nations (Matt 1:1–17; see D. A. Carson, *Matthew*, 63–69). Jesus is God with us, Immanuel, the ultimate fulfillment of Isaiah 7:14, according to Matthew 1:23.

I discuss the particulars of the beatitudes in other chapters in this volume. The remainder of this chapter will focus on characteristic features of Jesus' instruction. Three descriptive traits of Jesus' teaching are that he speaks authoritatively, paradoxically or counter-intuitively, and eschatologically or futuristically. In what follows, we will take up each of these statements. At the close of this chapter, we will return to Augustine's categories pertaining to happiness.

First, Jesus speaks *authoritatively;* his authority is not derivative, but original. Such authority manifests itself in the following: comparative statements like "You have heard that it was said . . . , but I say to you . . ." (e.g., Matt 5:21–22 and 5:27–28); Jesus' call to his hearers to build their lives on his teaching (Matt 7:24–27); and the authorial note at the conclusion to the Sermon on the Mount, ". . . when Jesus finished these sayings, the crowds were astonished at his teaching, for he was teaching them as one who had authority, and not as their scribes" (Matt 7:28–29). Perhaps most staggering in terms of his authority not being derivative, but rather original and ultimate, is Jesus' claim that his followers are like the prophets of old, as they suffer for him: "Blessed are you when others revile

---

Moreover, just as God called his Son Israel out of Egypt, so he calls Jesus his Son out of Egypt (Matt 2:15). The people of Israel were in the wilderness for forty years while Jesus was in the desert forty days and nights (Matt 4:2; the former disobeyed God during this period of testing, whereas Jesus obeyed). Regarding the reference in Matthew 5 to the mountain on which Jesus spoke, Carson does not see symbolic significance (129), though Robert Gundry does (see the reference to Gundry's work noted earlier). See for example his treatment of Matthew 5:1–10 in his *Commentary on Matthew.* Donald Hagner claims that the opening of the sermon is "carefully constructed": "(1) Jesus goes up to the mountain (a special place for a special event); (2) he sits down and his disciples come to him (as to a rabbinic master); and (3) in v 2, Matthew introduces the elaborate 'he opened his mouth and taught them, saying,' a construction that points to the weighty significance of what he is about to say." Hagner, *Matthew 1–13,* 85. Regardless of the significance of the reference to the mount, the Sermon on the Mount shows that Jesus speaks with an authority that is not imitative (he goes so far as to counter the traditions of men); his teaching originates with him (Matt 7:21–29). Moreover, Jesus recapitulates or transforms and perfects all of Israel's history, as its ultimate end or *telos* (Matt 5:17).

you and persecute you and utter all kinds of evil against you falsely on my account. Rejoice and be glad, for your reward is great in heaven, for so they persecuted the prophets who were before you" (Matt 5:11–12).

The thrust of Jesus' teaching being authoritative is that those who would be Jesus' disciples cannot engage in cut-and-paste antics of picking and choosing which portions of Jesus' teachings to obey. They are not convenient truths, but inconvenient and all-encompassing—Jesus demands our ultimate allegiance 24/7. The Beatitudes reflect the entire Sermon on the Mount and Jesus' entire corpus of teaching in their comprehensive call on our lives.

Second, not only is Jesus' teaching authoritative, but also it is *paradoxical* or *counter-intuitive*. The kingdom of heaven belongs to the poor in spirit, not those who are rich in their pride and autonomy (Matt 5:3). Those who mourn now will receive God's comfort; they will have the last laugh (Matt 5:4). The meek will inherit the earth, not those who run over others on their way to the top (Matt 5:5). We find in Jesus' teaching that he calls us to participate in an upside-down kingdom. While the kingdom is upside down from the world's vantage point, it is simply because the world perceives and interprets life wrongly. Actually, Jesus' kingdom is right-side up, and the world is upside down in its rebellion against God. In the end, all things will become clear. With this point in mind, it is worth drawing attention to a statement attributed to A. W. Tozer: "Man cannot say I am clever and Jesus is Lord at the same time." The wisdom of the world is foolishness to God and the way of the cross (1 Cor 1 and 2). Jesus' kingdom is counter-cultural at every turn; no wonder that is why John the Baptist prepares the way for Jesus with a baptism of repentance (Matt 3:1–3) and Jesus calls on people to repent in view of God's kingdom being at hand in his person, teaching, and miraculous activity (Matt 4:17, 23–25).

The thrust of Jesus' teaching being paradoxical or counter-intuitive is that we should not attempt to make sense of it according to other systems. Jesus' authoritative, paradoxical teaching is unique and stands alone. We cannot mix and match it with other systems; it binds us inseparably to him. Moreover, Jesus' teaching always calls us to repentance. Those who listen well to Jesus' teaching begin with a sense of their spiritual poverty (Matt 5:3), and never fail to sense their desperate need for God's wisdom and mercy. They realize their cleverness is nothing but a sham, and that they must become holy fools who become wise by adhering to Jesus' counter-cultural teaching.

Third, now we come to the *eschatological* nature of Jesus' teaching. We do not bring Jesus' future kingdom about by adhering to his teaching. Rather, Jesus ushers in his eschatological or future kingdom in our midst in his person. As we cling to him and despair of our religious merits and ingenuity in the here and now, we come to experience his kingdom blessings. In fact, it is his presence that causes us to despair of our merits and ingenuity (Matt 5:1–3). Moreover, we shall receive his comfort, grow in meekness, participate in his kingdom reign, and become satisfied, as we follow him (Matt 5:4–6).

The point of Jesus' teaching being eschatological is that we must not look at the kingdom with short-term thinking or in a near-sighted manner where we aim to attain the best of life in some truncated manner now. We must be marathon runners who see the big picture. In this world, Jesus' disciples will face many difficulties and persecution because of their union with him, as the Beatitudes make clear. We shall mourn, longing for comfort (Matt 5:4). We shall hunger and thirst for righteousness, longing to be filled (Matt 5:5). We shall be persecuted for righteousness, longing for God to make things right (Matt 5:10). The kingdom belongs to Jesus' followers, even though we await his kingdom's dramatic culmination.

In contrast to an individualistic and other-worldly spirituality, the Christian community is the concrete manifestation of the inbreaking kingdom. However, the community does not exhaust the kingdom. There is eschatological remainder. We have hope in Christ not only in this life, but in the kingdom to come in its fullness here on earth, thus guarding against pity and despair (1 Cor 15:19). There is hope in that this world order is not as good as it gets. Jesus' future and counter-cultural kingdom breaks into the present and informs us that those who live upside down now with him will be living rightside up then.

In view of the inaugurated *and* impending nature of the heavenly kingdom, Jesus' true disciples pursue him with an undying love and hold firmly to his teaching here and now, comforted by the fact that Jesus holds them firmly in his grip. They are truly happy, blessed, and honored, as they await the fullness of his kingdom with eager expectation. They know even now as they mourn that in Jesus they will have the last joyful laugh.

To return to Augustine's categories noted at the outset of this chapter, Jesus' followers may be persecuted for righteousness, but they are *not tortured* in spirit. They really will experience his eschatological kingdom's fullness, for which they long. Jesus' kingdom belongs to them. God has *not cheated* Jesus' disciples, for nothing else compares. His authoritative and paradoxical teaching sets it apart as original and ultimate. Jesus' subjects' passion is contagious, but it is *no disease* that makes it impossible for them to choose the good. They have sold everything to obtain Jesus and his kingdom, and will not discard him, but will share Jesus with everyone who catches their passion. What sets them all apart is that they know Jesus and his Father alone are good. Such subjects of the kingdom are truly happy and eternally blessed.

How does this discussion bear upon us? Like the people in Jesus' day, are we looking for happiness in all the wrong places? Have we observed happiness, but cannot attain it? Do we have it before us, but are unaware of the pearl of great price within our reach? Or do we have it in our possession, know it, and will not let it (him) go? If so, we are eternally blessed.

Cultural Reflection: Pull Yourself Up by the Bootstraps? I Don't Even Have Bootstraps!

As discussed above, tortured souls observe happiness, but cannot gain it. Cheated souls believe they have happiness, but are deceived. Diseased souls already have what should bring happiness, but they do not know it or seek it. Can you relate to any or all of these descriptions? I can. All of them. As a result, I really sense my need for Jesus as well as fellow followers to help me along the way.

From time to time, I think about the seed in the Parable of the Sower recorded in Matthew 13. I want to be like the seed sown on good soil, but my place of "rest" always appears to be on a turbulent path, on rocky ground, or among thorns. Here's the Lord Jesus' words:

> Hear then the parable of the sower: When anyone hears the word of the kingdom and does not understand it, the evil one comes and snatches away what has been sown in his heart. This is what was sown along the path. As for what was sown on rocky ground, this is the one who hears the word and immediately receives it with joy, yet he has no root in himself, but endures for a while, and when tribulation or persecution arises on account of the word, immediately he falls away. As for what was sown among thorns, this is the one who hears the word, but the cares of the world and the deceitfulness of riches choke the word, and it proves unfruitful. As for what was sown on good soil, this is the one who hears the word and understands it. He indeed bears fruit and yields, in one case a hundredfold, in another sixty, and in another thirty. (Matt 13:18–23)

I keep asking what will it take for me to be like the seed sown on the good soil recorded here.

To refer back to the Beatitudes, the seed sown on good soil is truly blessed. Though there are worries, temptations, tribulations, and persecution, the seed on good soil understands. He or she is not a tortured, cheated, or diseased soul.

Jesus is speaking to his disciples here, just as he did in the Sermon on the Mount. He called them. They didn't call him. They are blessed because he has revealed the secrets of the kingdom to them (Matt 13:11).

While I can make every effort to be the faithful follower that bears a hundredfold fruit, I just cannot make it happen. Certainly, I have a role to play. But without Jesus, I am doomed to fail. Thankfully, I did not call him, but he called me. Gratefully, he is not finished with me yet. Appreciatively, he has given me his Spirit and a community of fellow followers to help me on the way.

I am blessed to know that the very first beatitude is addressed to those who do not have "sufficient" bravado to pull themselves up by the bootstraps to attain the blessed life. In fact, they don't even have bootstraps! They are blessed because they know they're in great need of help. They are poor in spirit (Matt 5:3). They need Jesus to raise them up, and they need others whom he has also called to encourage and exhort them along the way.

Each of the biblical meditations that follow in the various chapters seek to unpack the Beatitudes. At the close of each biblical meditation, you will find cultural reflections that draw attention to people I know who help me along the path in pursuit of Jesus and his kingdom vision. These various individuals, and a host of others, encourage and exhort me through their lives. Without Jesus and his people, I could not ever hope to attain the blessed life.

I close this reflection with consideration of a friend named Tony. Tony is a very talented and thoughtful person. By his own admission, he is also a tortured soul. He's also cheated himself from time to time on his spiritual journey. But I think he is coming to terms with the fact that he is a very blessed man who is loved by God and those dearest to him.

It wasn't always this way. As I said, he has cheated himself from time to time. Once when asked to introduce himself at a gathering, he could not even bring himself to say he was a "Christ-follower," as had other disciples of Jesus gathered there. Rather, he said, "The Lord is my Shepherd. I shall not want." Perhaps like Peter with all his bravado and seeming spiritual brilliance (Matt 26:30–35; cf. Matt 16:13–23), but who came crashing down on the night of Jesus' betrayal and passion unto death with his denial (Matt 26:69–75), this fellow lamb realized his great need for Jesus in view of a recent spiritual and moral failure. Like Peter of old, it crushed him (Matt 26:75). I have always loved and admired this tortured, cheated, and sometimes diseased soul. He is so real, so tangible, so broken and in need of Jesus and others, so much like me. So much like you?

Lord Jesus, you are my Shepherd. Carry me. I don't even have bootstraps to pick myself up with. Give me companions for the journey to comfort, challenge, and encourage me. Together, may we enter your blessed rest.

Questions

1. When you think of the happy and blessed life apart from consideration of the Beatitudes, what do you envision?

2. Describe the substance and style of Jesus' teaching in the Beatitudes. What does his teaching content and delivery convey to you? How does his presentation of the happy or blessed life compare with your own? Please be specific.

3. Do you ever feel like a tortured, cheated, or diseased soul? If so, in what concrete ways?

4. Are you ever tempted to try and pick yourself up by the bootstraps and do the spiritual life on your own? What does that look like? How does that turn out usually for you?

5. Can you relate to Tony's story? If so, in what ways?

6. What would it be like for you to look to Jesus and others for help on your spiritual journey in seeking to live the happy or blessed life?

2

"Blessed Are the Poor in Spirit"
—Not Those with Spiritual Bravado

Biblical Meditation

I suppose it is easy for many people to feel a sense of superhuman capability when entering the New Year. After all, a new year of life brings confidence and hope and new beginnings. Couple this with the American "can-do-anything" attitude and one can feel like Superman or Superwoman. And, indeed, a sense of optimism and an unconquerable spirit certainly have their place and can be of great help when facing significant obstacles and overwhelming odds.

Against this backdrop, it might appear deeply counter-intuitive and confusing to hear Jesus' opening words in the Sermon on the Mount: "Blessed are the poor in spirit, for theirs is the kingdom of heaven" (Matt 5:3). The late John R. W. Stott explained that "poor in spirit" conveys the idea of "spiritual bankruptcy."[1] Those who are blessed before God are those who sense their spiritual bankruptcy. They are paupers in desperate need of God to bail them out. Jesus may have in mind Isaiah 61:1 (from which he quotes in Luke 4 in referring to God's calling on his life) and Isaiah 66:2:

1. Stott, *The Message of the Sermon on the Mount*, 39.

> The Spirit of the Lord God is upon me, because the Lord has anointed me to bring good news to the poor; he has sent me to bind up the brokenhearted, to proclaim liberty to the captives, and the opening of the prison to those who are bound. (Isa 61:1)

> All these things my hand has made, and so all these things came to be, declares the Lord. But this is the one to whom I will look: he who is humble and contrite in spirit and trembles at my word. (Isa 66:2)

God delights in those who sense their desperate need for God and his word (e.g., Ps 51:16–17). One of the things that God despises most is spiritual pride, which involves a smug sense of having arrived. Such spiritual pride grieves and quenches God's Spirit's working powerfully in our midst. It is like spiritual Kryptonite in our lives. God's Spirit acts on behalf of those who sense they have not arrived and await God's merciful intervention. Matt Woodley puts it this way: God "will pour out his Spirit wherever he finds open, thirsty, and desperate hearts. Our wealth, our education, our impressive programs and palatial buildings won't help us because when God finds poor-in-spirit, hungry, merciful people, he will display his power among them (see Matt 5:3–10)."[2]

This beatitude in Matthew 5:3 launches Jesus' State of the Union address for his kingdom that has just dawned (Matt 4:17). I wonder how someone like Peter responded to these word. After all, he sometimes had a certain kind of spiritual bravado about him, which Jesus would later extinguish through his gracious and merciful challenge (John 21:15–19). Jesus' opening words here in the Sermon on the Mount are also grace-filled—"Jesus blesses the spiritually *in*adequate," as Frederick Dale Bruner claims.[3] Do we sense our need for Jesus and his grace?

Jesus' state of the union address raises probing questions for us concerning the state of our union with him as we embark upon every new year and each new day. If we are to participate in Jesus' kingdom mission, it will begin and end with a radical sense of

2. Woodley, *The Gospel of Matthew,* 42.

3. Bruner, *Matthew: The Christbook,* 161.

dependence on his gracious character and his every word, as expressed in Matthew 5:3. As Bruner argues, "The purpose of every Command in the Sermon on the Mount is to drive its hearers back to this First Beatitude."[4]

The crowds were looking to Jesus. His disciples hoped in him and hung on his every word for life (Matt 5:1–2; cf. John 6:66–68). What about us today?

Cultural Reflection: What Does Spiritual Poverty Look Like When Filing for Bankruptcy Won't Help You Unless You're Donald Trump?

A *Forbes* 2011 article titled, "Fourth Time's a Charm: How Donald Trump Made Bankruptcy Work for Him," explains how Donald Trump was able to solve bankruptcy several times and still be a multi-billionaire. Two items the author notes are that Trump's name brand helped him as well as that he insulated himself personally much of the time. Apart from his first experience with bankruptcy, his personal fortune was not at stake.[5] Most of us are not so astute in navigating the system or have the name brand recognition and worth to keep financial stakeholders loaning and investing in us.

Just see what happens if you tell a banker that you are bankrupt. I spoke with a banker named Jennifer, whose financial institution has a credit rating of A, which means they rarely fail when it comes to debts because they are exceptionally conservative when loaning to customers. Jennifer told me that in her world "bankruptcy is the equivalent of a financial scarlet letter." Her bank will not touch someone who has claimed bankruptcy for seven years. While she cannot discourage someone for applying for credit, she and her colleagues hate to take an application from someone who has claimed bankruptcy. It is a waste of her time, since her bank will automatically decline lending to the person. In that case, the

4. Ibid.

5. O'Connor, "Fourth Time's A Charm."

individual in question only has one option available to them: find an institution willing to take a risk, which will involve the high probability of being taken advantage of with high interest rates.

Financial bankruptcy entails not having anything to secure debt, not even a trustworthy promise to ensure that you will repay. In that case, who will invest in you? Jennifer goes out of her way to keep people with major debt from maxing out their opportunities to borrow and falling into bankruptcy. It is a tragic irony that her supervisors encourage her to keep loaning to people even if they will plunge further and further into the abyss of debt until they reach bankrupt bottom. She has even taken a hit financially by refusing to loan to a customer who was on the near inevitable path to bankruptcy. Her boss simply transferred the application to another banker who processed the form and gave the man the loan, thereby benefiting the bank and the banker's own quota.

Jennifer is keenly able to spot hypocrisy a mile away in the business codes of her financial institution as well as institutional religion. As a Christian leader and pastor's wife, she sees inconsistencies as we quote God's spiritual codes in the church but cover our bases and refuse to confess when we fail to live them out. All too often, we fail to come clean on making public our spiritual tax returns. What do we have to hide? Jennifer and her husband have faced difficulties in church based on their integrity and honesty. As a result of their integrity and honesty inside and outside church, they have struggled to keep their family in the black financially. Moreover, they are transparent in their struggle to take to heart the red-letter words of Jesus, including the need to be poor in spirit (Matt 5:3) to gain credit with God.

Jennifer thinks I am overestimating her spiritual poverty or bankruptcy. This just goes to show that those who are truly poor in spirit do not realize it. Otherwise, they would boast in their extreme state of spiritual depth and not sense how truly desperately they are for God.

As Stott claimed in his exposition on Matthew 5:3, being poor in spirit means being spiritually bankrupt.[6] These are the

---

6. Stott, *The Message of the Sermon on the Mount*, 39.

only people whom God will bless. God does not bless those who think they are spiritually rich in themselves, only those who sense they have nothing with which to secure God's mercy and grace—not even a religious family's name.

Jennifer and her family face many struggles when it comes to being salt and light in the world of banking and the church. Being salt and light comes with a spiritual price tag—including persecution in religious institutions, sometimes a financial one, too. Even so, I believe Jennifer and her husband have an open line of credit with God for an abundance of grace and mercy because they remain spiritually poor.[7] Perhaps it's no coincidence that the first beatitude is on spiritual poverty (Matt 5:3) and the last beatitude is on persecution (Matt 5:10). Suffering often serves as a fast track to getting back on one's feet with spiritual solvency, as it can lead us to sense our need for God. As with bankruptcy, spiritual poverty comes with a price tag.

Questions

1. Having read the meditation on Matthew 5:3 and this reflection on bankruptcy, why do you think Jesus starts off the Beatitudes with a statement on the importance of poverty in spirit in the kingdom of God?

2. Might there be a connection between spiritual poverty (Matt 5:3) and persecution (Matt 5:10) for spiritual integrity? How do you explain that these are the bookends to the Beatitudes?

3. How often does financial security help or hinder sensitivity to our need for God?

---

7. To be clear, the abundance of God's gracious and merciful presence is truly the essence of the "blessed" or "happy" life despite the persecution one might face. Experiencing God's presence is a blessing that can't be matched by "feel good" or Instagram blessed expectations. Those seemingly great expectations only leave us hungry for more, never truly satisfied.

4. How often have you met people who are financially rich and yet embody Jesus' words of being spiritually poor? Why do you think they are often not correlated?

5. Do financial difficulties necessarily entail being spiritually poor? Why or why not?

6. How comfortable are you being spiritually poor? Why? What does spiritual poverty look like in your situation?

7. How might you learn from Jennifer and seek to help people stay out or get out of financial poverty, even at personal cost, and be transparent about the need for spiritual poverty, even at great cost?

8. Spiritual poverty is like humility. Those who are spiritually poor don't know they are, like Jennifer, just like those who think they are humble aren't. So, how do you become truly spiritually poor and humble in spirit if you will never know when you have acquired this trait?

3

"Blessed Are Those Who Mourn"
—Not Those Who Are Spiritually Comfortable

Biblical Meditation

Have you heard the expression, "God comforts the afflicted and afflicts the comfortable"? It does not originate from Jesus. Rather, it originates from journalism. According to blogger Tim Stewart, journalists referenced it in terms of the

> "watchdog" role that they felt newspapers were obligated to have. To journalists, the "afflicted" were the victims of crime or corruption in the big city. The "comfortable" were the fat cats in business and politics who were dabbling in crime and corruption behind the scenes. The journalists saw their dual role in the media as both comforting the victims of corruption and also calling the sleazy fat cats to account for their crimes.[1]

1. Stewart, "God Comforts the Afflicted and Afflicts the Comfortable." For the full discussion regarding the origin, evolution, and contextualization of this expression to religion, see Stewart's website (http://www.dictionaryof-christianese.com/god-comforts-the-afflicted-and-afflicts-the-comfortable), including his claim that Martin Marty was the first to contextualize the phrase to religion in a 1987 article (a respondent stated that there is an earlier religious application of the imagery in a tribute to Dorothy Day at Notre Dame).

Stewart remarks that the expression was created by Chicago journalist Finley Peter Dunne, not Joseph Pulitzer or H. L. Mencken, as others have claimed. Dunne referenced it in his column using a fictional character Mr. Dooley to speak of the events of the day in the colloquial voice of the common man:

> Th' newspaper does ivrything f'r us. It runs th' polis foorce an' th' banks, commands th' milishy, conthrols th' ligislachure, baptizes th' young, marries th' foolish, comforts th' afflicted, afflicts th' comfortable, buries th' dead an' roasts thim aftherward (*Observations by Mr. Dooley* (1902, 240)).[2]

Regardless of the interesting origin and evolution of the expression, it bears upon our present reflection on Matthew 5:4: "Blessed are those who mourn, for they shall be comforted" (Matt 5:4). This biblical expression, which many believe originates with Jesus, often *de*volves in our present context to read, "Blessed are the comfortable, for they will never mourn." If we are honest, many of us—including me—are tempted to prize consumer comfort in the religious and secular domain over most anything.

Jesus spoke in the voice of the common person to the all-too-common concerns of people's heart passions and imaginations in his day and our own. Those who are spiritually comfortable and smug do not mourn their true spiritual state. As the preceding beatitude in Matthew 5:3 indicates, those who are poor or bankrupt in spirit are blessed. They realize their desperate need for the God revealed in Jesus (see chapter 2). They mourn over their true spiritual condition and the spiritual darkness in the world.

Jesus calls those who mourn blessed; he promises that they will be comforted. Mourning is a mark of the true disciple. As Dietrich Bonhoeffer writes of Matthew 5:4, "Blessed are they that mourn, for they shall be comforted. . . . With each beatitude the gulf is widened between the disciples and the people, their call to come forth from the people becomes increasingly manifest."[3] Jesus' disciples

---

2. Ibid.

3. Bonhoeffer, *The Cost of Discipleship*, 108.

do "without what the world calls peace and prosperity."[4] They do not "accommodate" themselves to the world's "standards."[5] "While the world keeps holiday," Jesus' disciples "stand aside." "And while the world sings, 'Gather ye rose-buds while ye may,' they mourn."[6] "The Comforter of Israel" comforts them through his cross.[7] He is their comfort and rest as they align themselves with him, throwing themselves upon him, taking up his yoke. The rest Jesus promises is the rest of sharing in his burden, carrying his yoke. It is indeed rest, for when Christ is Lord in their place he bears the brunt of the burden (Matt 11:28–30).

The disciples are not absorbed in self-pity. They do not hate their neighbors and fellow citizens. In fact, as Bonhoeffer argues in this context in *The Cost of Discipleship* and models with his life, no one loves humanity more than Jesus and his true disciples. As Bonhoeffer argues in *Letters and Papers from Prison*, Jesus is the man for others, and the church is Jesus' community for others—*all* others.[8] The church bears witness to Jesus, who is the ultimate watchdog who comforts the afflicted and afflicts the comfortable.

Bonhoeffer mourned his own spiritual condition as well as the state of the German Christians, whom he opposed in their alignment with Hitler. He grieved for the extreme sorrow of the Jewish community and others whom Hitler exterminated, and he gave his life to try and bring an end to the Nazi menace. For Bonhoeffer, one cannot sing or rejoice in Christ who does not cry out for the Jewish community in their suffering: "Only he who cries out for the Jews may sing Gregorian chants."[9]

Jesus' comfort and joy does not entail silliness and sappiness that ignores the plight of the world bound up with sin and evil. Nor does Jesus' mourning entail sourness. Those engulfed in

4. Ibid.

5. Ibid.

6. Ibid.

7. Ibid., 109.

8. See Bonhoeffer's discussion of these themes in *Letters and Papers from Prison*, 381–86.

9. Marrus, ed., *The Nazi Holocaust*, 1401.

bitterness and morbidity readily forget the comfort that he alone brings. Those who grieve will be comforted, for the crucified and risen Jesus will bring an end to suffering.

What do you and I mourn over? Where do we find comfort? Do we mourn over our desire for comfort, which so often entails or ignores the suffering of others? Do we find comfort in the fact that the Jesus who was afflicted calls us to mourn with him so that we can find comfort in the joy of his resurrected presence that upholds us and makes all things new? Not unlike journalists who have a watchdog role to comfort the victims of corruption and afflict the victimizers, we must watch over our own hearts and bear witness to Jesus who comforts the afflicted and afflicts the comfortable.

Cultural Reflection: What Does Mourning Have to Do with Happiness and Clowning Around?

Can one be happy or blessed all the time? Is happiness the same thing as clowning around? Can one be happy and mourn simultaneously? If we think of happiness or blessedness as a perpetual state of being that is equivalent to clowning around all the time, then there's no occasion for mourning. If, however, we think of happiness or blessedness as a state of being in which one responds appropriately to life circumstances, then there would be occasions when mourning is appropriate, indeed blessed, and clowning around is not. In this case, Matthew 5:4 does not come across as a bad joke: "Blessed are those who mourn, for they shall be comforted."

Would you go to a funeral service for someone killed in a tragic event and clown around during the memorial? I hope not. It would be utterly inappropriate. Would you act silly and crack a bunch of jokes when someone's telling you they just received word they're dying of cancer? I doubt it. At least, not if you're emotionally intelligent.

In the face of challenging life circumstances, I look back with feelings of happiness and a sense of being blessed by having loved ones and friends who have identified with me in my grief rather than clown around. I can only hope and pray that I respond similarly to them when they go through dark times.

My friend Trudi is a clown as well as a pastor. Her clown's name is Nellie. Her pastor's name is Trudi. Trudi's one of the most relationally astute people I know. In my experience, she responds appropriately and empathically to people's various emotional states. She exemplifies emotional intelligence.

Given that I've used the term "emotional intelligence" a few times already, it would be good to define it. So, what's emotional intelligence? According to *Psychology Today*,

> Emotional intelligence is the ability to identify and manage your own emotions and the emotions of others. It is generally said to include three skills: emotional awareness; the ability to harness emotions and apply them to tasks like thinking and problem solving; and the ability to manage emotions, which includes regulating your own emotions and cheering up or calming down other people.[10]

In her work as a pastor and as a clown, Trudi's aware of her emotional surroundings, harnesses her own emotions well as she applies them to various tasks, and helps others regulate their own. I've been the beneficiary of her emotional skill set on various occasions!

If one thinks of clowns or pastors as silly or scary creatures, then one will miss out on key qualities that Trudi and Nellie embody. As a pastor and as a clown, my friend helps others come to terms with their life situations, drawing close and drawing out from them fitting emotional responses to their circumstances.

Take mourning, for example. As a pastor, Trudi discerns the importance of encouraging people to become aware of their need to mourn in view of their spiritual brokenness and that of the world. After all, if Jesus is a man of sorrows, familiar with suffering, grieving deeply while taking on the sin of the world (Isa 53:3–6), shouldn't we mourn, too? When we respond appropriately to

10. *Psychology Today*, "Emotional Intelligence."

our spiritual surroundings and state, we are blessed. We are also blessed when we apply appropriately emotional responses to tasks at hand. What do such appropriate applications look like? Those who are poor in spirit (Matt 5:3) and who mourn their spiritual poverty (Matt 5:4) will be meek toward others (Matt 5:5). They will also hunger and thirst for God's righteousness (Matt 5:6). The other beatitudes come into view here as well. Lastly, we are blessed if we regulate our emotional state and cheer or calm others, as the need arises, so that we live into the fullness of Jesus' kingdom mission. Trudi assists those around her to live the blessed life, even as she helps them mourn appropriately—not beating themselves up or down, but despairing of any attempts to save themselves, looking only unto Jesus to secure them.

Clowns like Trudi's Nellie don't always have to be silly to help people be happy. Nor do pastors like Trudi have to be upbeat all the time to help people experience blessedness. But they do have to understand when mourning is appropriate, how to harness it for navigating life circumstances well, and how to regulate emotions so that they do not take us too high or too low. The appropriate emotional state leaves us just right: right where Jesus would have us—centered in him in his kingdom of beatitudes.

Questions

1. How does mourning (Matt 5:4) relate to poverty of spirit (Matt 5:3)? How does mourning relate to meekness (Matt 5:5)?

2. How does mourning as envisioned by Jesus safeguard against the extremes of morbidity and silliness?

3. Sullenness and darkness shape the mood of some cultural movements, whereas sappiness frames others. How do you navigate between these extremes by coming alongside others to support them when they rejoice and when they mourn? What does emotional intelligence have to do with spiritual discernment in this context?

4. How do we move beyond a mindset of seeking to be comfortable at every turn in our Christian walk so that like Trudi/Nellie we might comfort others?

5. In Western culture, it is quite easy to think that those who are spiritually mature never feel sad but are always upbeat. Is this accurate? Why or why not, based on your reading of Matthew 5:3–4?

6. How does Jesus' life story and presence help us engage our sorrow and mourn in an anointed manner? What does "anointed" mourning look like?

4

"Blessed Are the Meek"
—Not Those Who Are Easily Provoked

Biblical Meditation

*ALERT: This chapter may contain spoilers of the movie,
Selma. The biblical content referenced here may also spoil
our desire to rule over others.*

Those who take themselves too seriously are easily slighted,
they are not meek. Jesus says, "Blessed are the meek, for they
shall inherit the earth" (Matt 5:5). The meek are not easily provoked. Following on from the preceding beatitudes in Matthew
5, those who are poor in spirit mourn their sinful, fragile, and
broken state; such awareness makes them meek. This progression
reminds me of David of old. David did not react to Shimei's ridi-
cule when he fled from Absalom's revolt, which was bound up with
the aftermath of David's own sin (2 Sam 16:5–14). All the more
significant is Jesus, who though pure and innocent is the epitome
of being meek, humble, and gentle (Matt 11:29). Jesus was not and
is not easily angered, though he was often slighted during his life
on earth (see the prophetic allusion of Isa 53:7). Even on the cross,

he asked his Father to forgive those who were responsible for his crucifixion (Luke 23:24).

If Jesus were easily angered, what would become of me? The thought of his mercy should be enough to make me poor in spirit, mournful, and meek. It should also cause me to hunger and thirst for real righteousness, not petty pound-of-flesh retributive repayments. The negative cycle of the latter never really ends.

One should not take from this reflection that the meek are doormats. If anything, those who are easily provoked are subject to the rule of others. People rule over those who are easily angered, as they react quickly, even to minor offenses. Albert Barnes offers a helpful reflection on this subject in his treatment of Matthew 5:5 in *Notes on the Bible*: "Meekness is patience in the reception of injuries. It is neither meanness nor a surrender of our rights, nor cowardice; but it is the opposite of sudden anger, of malice, of long-harbored vengeance."[1] Meekness is not weakness. According to Wayne Jackson in the *Christian Courier*, "'meek' is from the Greek term *praus*. It does not suggest weakness; rather, it denotes strength brought under control. The ancient Greeks employed the term to describe a wild horse tamed to the bridle" (italics added).[2] Frederick Dale Bruner makes this point clearly when he writes:

> Zealots of all types have never liked this blessing of the weak. For example, both social and capital enterprises (and their toadies, the success and assertiveness seminars) are far from praising the unaggressive, the timid, or those who do not claim all they can get: it is the aggressive, not the meek, who inherit their earth. It is those who push, who (in the favorite word in the literature) *struggle*, who get their piece of land. "For no one possesses this earth here below by gentleness, but only by pride" (Jerome, 1:106). Thus for a third time in three Beatitudes it appears that Jesus simply picks up the pieces. First to the dependent poor, then to the grief-stricken, and now to the unaggressive, Jesus gives everything: God's kingdom, God's comfort, and now God's green earth. Yet everyone

1. Barnes, *Notes on the New Testament*, 44.
2. Jackson, "Meek Inherit the Earth," lines 9–11.

else knows that it is the psychically and spiritually self-confident, the positive- and possibility-thinkers, and the dynamically assertive who really get things and who get things done on earth. The meek may inherit heaven—both the entrepreneur and the revolutionary will give the meek heaven—but not earth. Yet Jesus gives them earth.[3]

During his trial before the high priest, Jesus spoke up firmly and in a controlled manner when he was struck unjustly: "If what I said is wrong, bear witness about the wrong; but if what I said is right, why do you strike me?" (John 18:23). Although he was silent before Pilate during his execution trial, he spoke up in a similar manner when Pilate warned him of his authority to have Jesus executed. Jesus corrected Pilate. In other words, he put him in his place. Jesus answered Pilate, "You would have no authority over me at all unless it had been given you from above. Therefore he who delivered me over to you has the greater sin" (John 19:11, see the entire context of verses 1–6).

Jesus spoke up for what was right and just; he did not speak out regarding minor offenses of personal fancy. How do we know that we are not petty in our grievances, but profound? We embody profound values when we take offense against injustice. Concern for justice is vitally important. Justice entails rightful concern for God's honor and acknowledgment of God's kingdom authority, as when Jesus rebuked Pilate. It also showed in Jesus' concern for the people. When we don't care for those in need, we don't care for Jesus, who always speaks out against injustice on behalf of the discounted and exploited (Matt 25:31–46). Again, Bruner forcefully demonstrates this point:

> Jesus himself is the best definition of meekness, particularly at his trial (Matt 26–27). We do not exactly see weakness there, but we do not see many claims there either, and not a great deal of aggression. The overall impression of Jesus on trial is an impression of poise. It is the poise of not having to assert oneself. It is the poise, if I may put it this way, of a believer. There is a meekness

3. Bruner, *Matthew: The Christbook*, 161.

that is almighty and a gentleness that is strong. In a world threatened by terrorist holocaust macro-cosmically and by the destruction of the family microcosmically, the great need of the age may be this Beatitude's gentle-men and gentle-women. The Third Beatitude's little people may well be the hope of the earth, though the rest of the world tells us that the real hope of the earth is the big people and the earth shakers.[4]

The Baptist minister Dr. Martin Luther King Jr. spoke out against injustices against an oppressed people. He also showed evidence of shrugging off the slights committed against him. These qualities came through in the movie *Selma*, which my wife and I went to see when it appeared in theaters. The movie chronicles critical events surrounding King and the people's struggle in the Civil Rights movement in 1965 in Selma, Alabama. The historic march from Selma to Montgomery climaxed in President Johnson's signing of the Voting Rights Act that year. For King, the gospel compelled him to lead a movement for justice birthed in the African American church in a non-violent manner.

The movie *Selma* shows King's colleague Andrew Young explaining to someone wishing to react violently to their oppressors that the people would not have stood a chance if they had resorted to guns and violence against the unjust authorities at Selma. Their only chance to win rights was to operate in a non-violent manner. Above and beyond the strategic wisdom of this approach in contending against an overwhelming unjust force, King grounded the movement and approach in Jesus' love ethic. King believed that such love was not simply essential to bringing about reconciliation between individuals, but also critical to effecting social transformation on a massive scale.[5]

One should not think that Jesus or King's meek, non-retaliatory approach toward one's oppressors entails groveling in the dirt. In Jesus' day, turning the other cheek toward one's oppressor did not rob people of their dignity. It caused the offending party

---

4. Ibid.

5. See Carson, *The Autobiography of Martin Luther King, Jr.*, 23–24.

to have to look at those they slapped as equals. The slapping of someone on the right cheek most likely entailed in Jesus' context a humiliating strike with the backside of the right hand intended for an inferior. If the person intended to strike again, the offer of the left cheek repositioned the conflict as one between equals.[6] In the Civil Rights era, King and his movement did not stoop to the inhumanity of their oppressors. The injustice they endured served to prick the American conscience, as multitudes of people witnessed via the national news the horrors committed by those seeking to enforce segregation and inequality. In view of Jesus and his servant, King, those who think they are superior to those they oppress need to realize that only by becoming meek do they become truly human.

As early as 1957,[7] King spoke of such non-violent confrontation grounded in love. Here is what King said in a sermon at Christmas in 1967 at Ebenezer Baptist Church,

> Somehow we must be able to stand up to our most bitter opponents and say: "We shall match your capacity to inflict suffering by our capacity to endure suffering. We will meet your physical force with soul force. Do to us what you will and we will still love you. We cannot in all good conscience obey your unjust laws and abide by the unjust system, because noncooperation with evil is as much a moral obligation as is cooperation with good, and so throw us in jail and we will still love you. Bomb our homes and threaten our children, and, as difficult as it is, we will still love you. Send your hooded perpetrators of violence into our communities at the midnight hour and drag us out on some wayside road and leave us half dead, and we will still love you. . . . But be assured that we'll wear you down by our capacity to suffer, and one day we will win freedom. We will not only win freedom for ourselves; we will so appeal to your heart and

6. See Wright, *Matthew for Everyone*, 49–53.

7. For an example of King's consistent message of non-violence see the transcript to his sermon entitled, "Loving Your Enemies," given at Dexter Avenue Baptist Church on November 17, 1957. http://kingencyclopedia.stanford.edu/encyclopedia/documentsentry/doc_loving_your_enemies.

conscience that we will win you in the process, and our
victory will be a double victory."[8]

King's non-violent protest flowed from Jesus' call to love our enemies and pray for those who persecute us (Matt 5:44). The late
Evangelical Anglican statesman John R. W. Stott claimed that King
was the greatest model of Jesus' ethic disclosed in this text in the
modern age.[9]

King and company witnessed President Johnson's action on
their behalf, as he eventually signed the Voting Rights Act in 1965.
Perhaps many in the Civil Rights movement felt at the signing of
the law that they were on their way to inherit the earth. Certainly
Jesus had in mind the eventual restoration of all things at the end
of history in his kingdom reign, when he spoke of the meek inher-
iting the earth. Still, the Civil Rights reform of 1965 bore witness
to that just state of affairs at the end of history and foreshadowed
it in some way. When we are meek, not weak, working on behalf
of Jesus' just kingdom, sensing our desperate need for Jesus' intervention, and mourning our sinful condition and that of the world,
we can take comfort in knowing that we will inherit the earth.

How do you and I want to go down in history? Do we want to
rise up with the just or go down with the unjust, up with the meek
or down with those who promote an unjust peace? Psalm 37:10–11
declares, "In just a little while, the wicked will be no more; though
you look carefully at his place, he will not be there. But the meek
shall inherit the land and delight themselves in abundant peace"
(Ps 37:10–11).

President Johnson did not want history to see him taking
sides with Governor Wallace of Alabama on the critical events
surrounding Selma, as disclosed in the movie. Rather, he wanted
posterity to view him as being on the side of justice by siding with

8. In *A Testament of Hope*, 256–57.

9. Stott, *The Message of the Sermon on the Mount*, 113. On the ethical
significance of the Sermon on the Mount, see Scott McKnight's treatment of it
in relation to various ethical systems in *Sermon on the Mount*, 1–19. McKnight
refers to it as "the greatest moral document of all time." McKnight, *Sermon on
the Mount*, 2.

King's strong, resilient community of meekness. In the end, how will Jesus view *us*—as those on the side of cruel weakness or meek strength? Only the latter will inherit the earth.

Cultural Reflection: What Does Biblical Meekness Look Like in a Litigation-Loaded Culture?

John practices law and is a practicing Christian. Some might wonder how "practices law" and "practicing Christian" can go together in the same sentence, but John's story reveals that they can.

John was involved in a mediation proceeding with a former client based on a conflict between his law firm and this former client that dated back several years. John and his team sat in one room, and the other party and his lawyer sat in another. The mediator went back and forth asking questions to probe for veracity and to try and uncover inconsistencies in their respective testimonies.

John had asked me privately to pray for the mediation. The process can take numerous hours and be very draining. John had also shared that the client (whose name he did not offer) had given a very misleading and distorted account of the conflict for several years. The mediation would make it possible to set straight the record.

The day's proceedings were not going well. It seemed as if the tensions were only intensifying, as the two sides gave very different accounts to the legal mediator. However, late in the day, a breakthrough occurred. The former client came to an understanding that it would be in their best interest to settle and desist with the accusations, which John says were unfounded charges.

After it was all said and done, John's colleagues turned to John and asked him how he had prayed for the proceedings. They knew John was a Christian, and that he had prayed in preparation for the mediation. John responded by saying that he had prayed God's blessings on the former client prior to and during the proceedings, and that they would discern what is true and just. John's colleagues were surprised that he had not prayed for the other party's demise, or that John and his team would win. A prayer for blessing and discernment of truth and justice was all John prayed.

The moral of the story is not that those who pray meekly inherit the earth now. A similar mediation might go the other way. One never knows. But according to Matthew 5:5, the meek *will someday* inherit the earth. John shared with me that if he does not forgive his enemies and pray God's blessings on them, he cannot experience God's peace. *What earth would he inherit if he does not operate at every turn in meekness, gentleness, and humility, but instead oversteps his bounds and plays God?* One injustice would simply replace another. It is important to make one's case, but still entrust everything to the Almighty. It is *God's* place to judge, not John's, not yours, and not mine. As Jesus says elsewhere in the Sermon on the Mount,

> You have heard that it was said, "You shall love your neighbor and hate your enemy." But I say to you, Love your enemies and pray for those who persecute you, so that you may be sons of your Father who is in heaven. For he makes his sun rise on the evil and on the good, and sends rain on the just and on the unjust. For if you love those who love you, what reward do you have? Do not even the tax collectors do the same? And if you greet only your brothers, what more are you doing than others? Do not even the gentiles do the same? You therefore must be perfect, as your heavenly Father is perfect."
> (Matt 5:43–48)

Must not those who practice Christianity like John, an attorney at law, pursue justice in the same way as their Lord? Yes, Jesus will judge the nations (Matt 25:31–33), but he lived daily in a spirit of meekness, gentleness, and humility. We who call him Lord must do the same.

Questions

1. Having read the meditation on Matthew 5:5 and this reflection on John's deposition case, what do you think of when you

consider the term "meekness" in its application to following Jesus Christ?

2. How would you have prayed if you were in John's shoes? Are there other kinds of prayers that one could offer concerning the other party in the mediation?

3. Is it ever appropriate as a Christian to pray God's judgment on another person or party? If so, what biblical support might you offer for your position?

4. Can one take meekness "too far" as a Christian? If so, what might that look like?

5. In my estimation, John demonstrated meekness, which the biblical meditation above defines as strength under control rather than weakness. Rather than being easily provoked, he was patient and sought to see the big picture of God's impending just rule. What are some ways in which you guard against being easily provoked and submit everything to God's approaching just rule over the nations?

6. Dr. Martin Luther King Jr. spoke out against injustice even while operating meekly. He suffered many injustices to his person, including slander, the bombing of his home, personal blows, and eventual assassination. Still, his overarching heart cry was for marginalized people, not himself. How often do we cry out for justice to be served for the orphan, widow, and alien in their distress in comparison to our cries for others to treat us fairly?

7. Remember that Jesus is Lord of the kingdom, and that according to Jesus the meek will inherit the earth. How might these biblical claims encourage us to grow in meekness?

5

"Blessed Are Those Who Hunger and Thirst for Righteousness" —Not Those Who Crave Fast-food Justice

Biblical Meditation

Much of what passes for fast food never really satisfies. It leaves a hunger hole where one craves more. According to an article published in the *Daily Mail*,

> Research shows that unhealthy fats found in dairy products, burgers, and milk shakes quickly make their way to the brain, where they shut off the alarm system that tells us when we've had enough to eat.
>
> As a result our hunger is not satisfied, and we eat more and more.
>
> The effect is so powerful that a cheeseburger eaten on a Friday could be responsible for feelings of hunger three days later, the U.S. researchers believe.
>
> Dr. Deborah Clegg, who carried out the study, said: "Normally, our body is primed to say when we've had enough, but that doesn't always happen when we're eating something good.

"What we've shown in this study is that someone's entire brain chemistry can change in a very short period of time."

In a series of experiments, Dr. Clegg showed that saturated fats trick the body into switching off the system that tells us how hungry we are and whether we've eaten enough.[1]

Like fast food generally, fast-food righteousness can alter one's entire spiritual chemistry in short order. It shuts off the alarm system in our souls that tells us when we've had enough righteousness to eat. We remain hungry because the righteousness we are eating is high on saturated fats. The food is not quality and tricks us into thinking we have not had enough of it to eat. So we keep eating it.

So what is fast-food righteousness? What is righteousness that contains all kinds of saturated fats? It is the opposite kind of righteousness to that which we find Jesus promoting in Matthew 5:6: "Blessed are those who hunger and thirst for righteousness, for they shall be satisfied" (Matt 5:6). Fast-food righteousness includes self-righteousness, which entails taking matters into our own hands or wishing that others would take matters into their hands on our behalf. It also entails the sense that we are the ultimate decision makers on what is right and wrong. But the Greek word *dikaiosunē,* which we often translate as "righteousness," does not just pertain to the state of the self. It also includes "justice" in its meaning and as such refers to a state that ultimately demands equity for all. This will no doubt expand and reorient our thinking on such matters. Many, if not all of us, want quick action taken on our behalf rather than wait on God and look to God who alone is just and the ultimate arbiter of justice. It involves hate and revenge rather than love and mercy. It fixates on getting even with others rather than making things right. Others of us might appear passive. We might not demand quick righteousness or justice on our behalf. Still, we might permit a desire for revenge to grow within us. At some point that very passion might erupt unexpectedly.

1. Macrae, "Junk Food Alters Brain Chemistry."

Dr. King was often accused by the early Malcolm X and others of being passive and the pawn of white oppressors. But King was no pawn. He was not passive. He was active. He pursued a long-lasting course of just action bound up with the gospel of love. Love for King was coercive, destabilizing, and compelling in that it struck at the consciences of people in the depths of their being. King called for action. He called for active, tenacious, long-lasting love that would overwhelm the hate and indifference of oppression, as reflected in the following statement taken from "Where Do We Go from Here?" delivered on August 16th, 1967 in Atlanta, Georgia:

> And I say to you, I have also decided to stick to love. For I know that love is ultimately the only answer to mankind's problems. And I'm going to talk about it everywhere I go. I know it isn't popular to talk about it in some circles today. I'm not talking about emotional bosh when I talk about love, I'm talking about a strong, demanding love. And I have seen too much hate. I've seen too much hate on the faces of sheriffs in the South. I've seen hate on the faces of too many Klansmen and too many White Citizens Councilors in the South to want to hate myself, because every time I see it, I know that it does something to their faces and their personalities, and I say to myself that hate is too great a burden to bear. I have decided to love. If you are seeking the highest good, I think you can find it through love. And the beautiful thing is that we are moving against wrong when we do it, because John was right, God is love. He who hates does not know God, but he who loves has the key that unlocks the door to the meaning of ultimate reality.[2]

Hate shuts off the alarm system in our souls that tells us when we have gotten our fill of justice. Revenge is a fast-food form of justice that tells us to settle for poorly and hastily prepared righteousness. As long as it tastes great and takes care of the momentary ache in our spiritual guts, we think we will be satisfied. But we

2. In *A Testament of Hope*, 250.

won't. We will keep going back for more of the same and those we seek to repay will keep coming back to reciprocate.

One cannot take away the craving for true righteousness with poorly prepared, fast-food justice solutions. Fits of rage bent on revenge will not ultimately satisfy. Nor will the presumption of self-righteousness. Everyone wants to take justice into their own hands when it involves wrongs done to them, but we cry out for mercy when we are the ones in God's hands (e.g., Jesus' Parable of the Unforgiving Servant in Matt 18:21–35).

So, what kind of righteousness does not go down like fast food, but is rich in nutrients and good for the soul? You will find that the Bible's label of ingredients for righteousness is quite thorough and substantial. Let's take a look.

Those who crave God's righteousness are meek, not vigilantes. They are redemptive, not retributive in advancing justice concerns. They are like the Son of Man, not the Sons of Thunder (Luke 9:54–55). Jesus' mature followers do not crave fast-food justice. They are not quick to judge in view of a presumed sense of entitlement to take matters into their own hands. Moreover, they recognize that they themselves require mercy and grace. Later in the Sermon on the Mount (Matt 7:1–5), Jesus warns his listeners not to judge others, or else they will face judgment. They (we) must be ever mindful of their own spiritual need and total inability to serve as the ultimate standards of righteousness.

Jesus who is the arbiter of justice and righteousness alone knows what kind of righteousness will satisfy. He declares, "Blessed are those who hunger and thirst for righteousness, for they shall be satisfied" (Matt 5:6). The righteousness that he has in mind for us never turns off our alarm system that tells us when we have had enough justice to eat. He tells us that those who have never gotten their fill of being righted and hailed as righteous fail to account for their ultimate poverty of spirit, fail to mourn their spiritual state, and fail to comprehend their need for meekness. Righteousness ultimately derives from our union with Jesus—the Lord of the kingdom. Those who align themselves with Jesus will be satisfied.

Their hunger will be filled. Their thirst will be quenched. He will make all things right and whole.

Scripture emphasizes in different contexts declarative or legal righteousness and personal as well as social righteousness. For example, God justifies the ungodly and makes his people just and advocates of justice. Paul speaks often of God's righteousness (*dikaiosunē*). It often involves a declarative or legal sense bound up with our faith (e.g., Rom 4 and 5). In contradistinction, the Synoptic Gospels speak often of personal and social righteousness as required of God's people who believe (e.g., see what occurs when Zacchaeus repents and believes in Jesus in Luke 19:1–10).[3]

Personal righteousness and social righteousness go hand in hand in the Bible. There must be integrity in our lives between what we proclaim and how we live in our private and public spheres. Jesus' half-brother James blends the personal and public forms of righteousness when he writes, "Religion that is pure and undefiled before God, the Father, is this: to visit orphans and widows in their affliction, and to keep oneself unstained from the world" (Jas 1:27). Of course, Jesus was concerned for personal righteousness, as reflected in his utterances in the Sermon on the Mount to that effect. Such concern would also entail a prophetic challenge to religion framed socially as legalistic adherence to mere external forms. (See his statements on Pharisaical righteousness in Matt 5:17–20 and anger and lust in 5:21–30; see also Jesus' claims bearing on justice toward the oppressed and downtrodden among the nations in Matt 25:31–46.)

Cathy Deddo of the Trinity Study Center provides the following helpful reflection on righteousness in Matthew 5:6:

> What is righteousness? Often I think we assume it is the achievement of some perfect and unnatural state. But righteousness is simpler and far broader than that. Righteousness is having all things set right. When there is righteousness in the world then all things will be in

3. See D. A. Carson on righteousness involving *both* personal *and* social dimensions (though not imputation) in Matthew 5:6 in *The Expositor's Bible Commentary*, 134.

right relationship with one another and will be living and acting according to [their] created purpose[s]. To desire righteousness in ourselves is to desire that we are living in line with who we were created to be and not in rebellion to it. Jesus says here that one who is hungering for righteousness is blessed. This means that these people are those who ache to see things made right, in all places. The desire is so deep, so intense, that they feel they cannot live without it. The person that Jesus is talking about here is longing to see, for example, justice in the Middle East and relationships full of joy, blessing, and peace around them.[4]

Such concern for righteousness spans the Old and New Testaments. In a discussion on hunger, thirst, and satisfaction/filling bound up with righteousness in Matthew 5:6, it is worth meditating on fasting as it is presented in Isaiah 58. Isaiah 58 speaks of the kind of fasting that God requires. It involves sensing our spiritual need to act righteously on behalf of the poor rather than sitting back and getting fat on spiritual smugness bound up with religious practices that discount or ignore the poor. Just as I have found that regular exercise helps moderate my hunger and increases a healthy appetite, so too, I sense that God truly satisfies me when I exercise justice among those in need in dependence on him. Moreover, ministry among the poor and marginalized causes me to sense in increasing measure how great my own need is for him. I realize I cannot minister holistically apart from total dependence on him.

Ultimately, righteousness flows from Jesus, as Jesus himself declares. Contrary to those liberal Christians who claim that the one who preached became the one who was preached, Jesus preached himself. He is the Lord God of the kingdom and incarnate, authoritative embodiment of its values. Matthew 7:21–29 sets forth how the one who was preached and the one who preached are one. From the opposite end, contrary to those conservative Christians who claim that the one who was preached did not preach

4. Deddo, "Matthew 5:5–6," paragraph 12. See also N. T. Wright's article titled "Righteousness," 590–92. See also my article, "What Is Biblical Justice?" 25.

concern for injustices in society as a whole, Jesus is the ultimate social liberator.

Not everyone who proclaims justice operates justly and finds favor with Jesus. And yet, true justice, no matter where it is found, derives from Jesus, even in those places and among those people not explicitly aligned with him. For disciples of Jesus, though, our emphasis on justice derives from our hungering and thirsting for his righteousness to permeate all of our private lives, our personal and social transactions, and the entire world. As we seek to honor Jesus, we don't make ourselves the arbiters of justice. We don't try to take matters into our own hands. We understand that our ultimate filling awaits his kingdom's total realization. Yet, while we don't take matters into our own hands, we also challenge surface-level, fast-food versions of justice. We invite everyone to find their satisfaction in him, for we realize that Jesus' righteousness and justice is far more nutritious and sticks to the bones.

Cultural Reflection: Do You Take Clean Water for Granted? If So, How Will You Ever Hunger and Thirst for Righteousness?

It's easy to take clean water for granted in the United States, especially if you drink filtered and bottled spring water all the time. Did you know that nearly 700 million people across the world lack access to clean water? That's nearly 10 percent of the people on the planet.[5] Papua New Guinea has the worst clean water access.[6] It's one thing if you live in the gentrified Port Moresby, but if you live in the surrounding jungles your access to clean water is far worse. Sixty percent of the country's population don't have the means of purifying their water supply,[7] even though their water resources

5. World Health Organization, "Key Facts from JMP 2015 Report." Many thanks to Mark Nicklas for various relevant online resources.

6. Kweifio-Okai, "Papua New Guinea Has World's Worst Access to Clean Water, Says Water Aid."

7. World Health Organization/UNICEF, "Key Facts from JMP 2015 Report."

are abundant. This is no small matter, as disease and infant mortality rates have climbed dramatically, even as the urban poor have been forced to migrate to the jungle mountains.

A pastor among the mountain poor in Papua New Guinea named Magi invited a fellow pastor named Mark from Beaverton, Oregon to assist him and his people gain access to clean water. Mark and a lay leader in his church named Jim have expertise in the science and technology of water drilling and purification. However, they didn't go with an expert's attitude to lead a group of servants, but as servants with expertise to assist Magi and his people as the indigenous people saw fit. There's a major difference in the posture between the two approaches. Among other things, they did not intrude, but were invited. They learned from Magi and others what the situation entailed, and what would work best for them, and what skills and expertise they already had that could be drawn upon in assisting with water purification. Such education is truly equitable and righteous, not elitist.

I mentioned earlier that it's easy to take clean water for granted. Perhaps some of us also take righteousness and justice for granted. We're so blessed in America to have a legal system that is sound, even though we often fail to implement its ideals and procedures appropriately. However, I can't be blessed in the way that Jesus intends in Matthew 5:6 if I don't hunger and thirst for righteousness. Those who are truly hungry and thirsty never take their food and drink for granted. I've never been displaced from my home due to gentrification or other means. But as many Native Americans and African Americans can testify, gentrification is a real threat for them historically and presently. The same gentrified reality is painfully real for Magi and his people, as they had no other option than to move from the city to the surrounding jungles. Like many cities that have experienced urban renewal, Mark mentions that some hail Port Moresby's renewal as a great success story. "But for whom?" Mark asks. The displaced urban poor? Or the rich, the government, and Western corporate industries who have partnered with the government to renew the city and remove the poor? Just like the clean water, many of us—myself included—take our middle- and upper-class justice for granted.

Jesus' beatitude about hungering and thirsting for righteousness (Matt 5:6) was not lost on the hungry and thirsty people hanging on his every word. No doubt, many of them were living on daily bread without surplus in the fridge or even a filtered water dispenser in the fridge door. As much as Jesus fed the masses physically, as the Gospels record (Matt 14:13–21), he always exhorted the people to hunger and thirst for righteousness, which was also in short supply for them under Rome's oppressive rule.

As a pastor, Magi and his associates, with the help of Mark and Jim, are caring for people's physical and spiritual hunger and thirst. Magi doesn't take physical or spiritual food and drink for granted. He also understands that the former does not come with a promise of being filled, whereas the latter does (Matt 5:6). So, while the mortality rate is declining due to the clean water access they now have, Magi recognizes the huge gains they've made can dry up in an instant if those with money and power push them further into the jungle. And so, Magi's also helping his community find eternal sustenance, which no government or company can take away. That's nothing to take for granted. Let's take it to heart and drink to that.

Questions

1. How might the preceding beatitudes bear upon hungering and thirsting for righteousness? How might hungering and thirsting for righteousness bear upon the beatitudes that follow?

2. How easy is it for you to take clean water and food for granted? How about righteousness? How might you take it for granted?

3. Where does the idea come from that righteousness pertains only to "personal holiness"? Where does the idea come from that righteousness pertains only to "social justice"?

4. In light of Matthew's teaching on righteousness (including Matt 5:6) expounded in this particular biblical meditation,

and in light of this cultural reflection, how might you respond to those who think that righteousness pertains only to personal or social being, not both?

5. If Mark and Jim were about fast-food righteousness, how might it impact their engagement of Magi and the church in Papua New Guinea? If Magi were about fast-food righteousness, how might it affect him and his community?

6. How does self-righteousness relate to an "expert" or a Messiah complex in missions? How does God's righteousness relate to an "invited guest" approach to missions, which involves mutuality that draws on the expertise of all parties (for example, Mark and Jim, as well as Magi and his fellow Papua New Guineans)?

7. What does fast-food righteousness look like in your own experience? What does Jesus' kind of righteousness look like in your experience? Please give a concrete example of each.

8. How might our understanding of righteousness flowing from Jesus as Lord of the kingdom shape our approach to righteousness in our own lives, and in our engagement of others and society?

6

"Blessed Are the Merciful"
—Not Those Who Look Out
for Number One

Biblical Meditation

The Beatitudes are filled with paradoxes. For example, the kingdom belongs to the poor in spirit, not to those with spiritual bravado. The meek, not those who are easily provoked, will inherit the earth. Following these and other beatitudes, Jesus goes on to say, "Blessed are the merciful, for they shall receive mercy" (Matt 5:7). John Calvin writes of this beatitude:

> Happy are the merciful[:] This paradox, too, contradicts the judgment of men. The world reckons those men to be happy, who give themselves no concern about the distresses of others, but consult their own ease. Christ says that those are happy, who are not only prepared to endure their own afflictions, but to take a share in the afflictions of others,—who assist the wretched,—who willingly take part with those who are in distress,—who clothe themselves, as it were, with the same affections, that they may be more readily disposed to render them assistance. He adds, for they shall obtain mercy,—not only with God, but also among men, whose minds God

will dispose to the exercise of humanity. [368] Though the whole world may sometimes be ungrateful, and may return the very worst reward to those who have done acts of kindness to them, it ought to be reckoned enough, that grace is laid up with God for the merciful and humane, so that they, in their turn, will find him to be gracious and merciful ... (Ps 103:8; Ps 145:8).[1]

While it might appear paradoxical that people should be merciful, a merciful disposition naturally or supernaturally resonates with the very character of God. Moreover, it is not paradoxical but predictable that those who are merciful will receive mercy.

Having said this, those who pursue self-righteousness all too often snub their noses at those in need rather than show them mercy. It is as if they are saying, "It serves them right. They must be lazy.... It just goes to show that you reap what you sow." Those who come to terms with their spiritual state of extreme poverty (Matt 5:3) and who mourn their spiritual condition (Matt 5:4) are slow to pass judgment on others. In this same vein, they are not easily provoked when someone does them wrong (Matt 5:5). Rather than passing judgment, and positioning themselves as above judgment, they hunger to be filled with God's righteousness (Matt 5:6). They realize that their righteousness is hollow.

The truly merciful realize how indebted they are to God for his mercy, and so they show mercy to those in need. In turn, God shows them mercy over and over again: "Blessed are the merciful, for they shall receive mercy" (Matt 5:7). How we treat those in need serves as a barometer for how well we have accounted for God's mercy on display in our lives. Unlike the ungrateful and merciless servant, we should never cease to extend mercy and forgiveness toward others given how merciful God is toward us (Matt 18:21-35).

This discussion calls to mind *Les Misérables*, where Jean Valjean becomes a person who displays great mercy toward others as a result of experiencing the profound mercy of a Catholic bishop who does not turn him over to the authorities for clubbing and

---

1. Calvin, *New Testament Commentaries*, 171.

robbing him. I love the scene where the authorities bring Valjean (the former convict who had spent years in prison doing hard labor) back to the bishop's residence with the bishop's prized silver tableware, which they had found in Valjean's possession. Instead of accusing him of stealing the silver and sending him back to prison, the bishop tells the police that he had given the silver to Valjean and that Valjean had forgotten to take the silver candlesticks. He then gives Valjean the candlesticks. So, the police release Valjean. Left alone, the bishop tells a dumbfounded and confused Valjean that he no longer belongs to evil The bishop says that he has bought Valjean's soul and ransomed him from fear and hatred and has given him back to God. His profound act of mercy transforms Valjean. Later, Valjean even shows mercy to the police officer who spends years trying to hunt him down; Valjean's mercy toward the authority undoes him; this policeman (Javert) who believes that the law does not permit mercy kills himself.

Hugo gets at the heart of mercy and grace in this volume. On the back cover of my copy of *Les Misérables*, V. S. Pritchett is quoted as saying that Hugo conveys human nature in mythical proportions in service to poverty-stricken and oppressed souls. For Hugo, this volume was "a religious work," to which Pritchett adds, "it has indeed the necessary air of having been written by God in one of his more accessible and saleable moods."[2] If only we would not readily treat God's mercy toward humanity as myth, and see that mercy reflects God's dominant mood. It would be equally amazing if we were to treat our fellow humans mercifully in mythical proportions!

Only those who have experienced mercy factually—and not simply mythically in great works of fiction, and have taken God's mercy to heart—realize that they are not number one. They realize that the universe does not revolve around them. They comprehend that if it were not for the favor of others, whether God or fellow humans, they would not be alive today.

At the outset of this piece, I spoke about how the beatitudes are filled with paradoxes. There are also paradoxes in theology

2. Pritchett, back cover of *Les Misérables*.

and problems with our perceptions concerning God and the law. One of the many paradoxes revolves around the ultimate number one—God. All too often, we look at God as one who is easily provoked and lacking in mercy. We even think that the God of the Old Testament presents himself in this way. According to my colleague, Karl Kutz, Professor of Hebrew at Multnomah University, Exodus 33:18–19 and Exodus 34:5–7 unpack the self-defining God of Exodus 3:13–15 ("I am who I am"):

> God does not say, "I am." He says, "I am WHO I AM." The Hebrew seems to suggest that God is self-defining. God will be all that he is, *especially as it relates to our humanity and need.* This thought is vividly displayed in the description of Moses' encounter with God after the episode of the golden calf. (italics added)

After quoting Exodus 33:18–19 and Exodus 34:5–7, Kutz argues,

> These are not the things that perhaps first come to our mind when we think about defining the character of God. Perhaps we would have started with things like his holiness, transcendence, and immortality.
>
> Yet when God chooses to express his name *he chooses first and foremost to identify the attributes that meet us in the depths of our human need.* It is only at the end of this statement that he reminds us that he will not be part of who he is. His judgment of sin is equally a part of his character. This is the self-defining God. He is a God who will be all that he is. He is God who cannot be part of his essence. *He is God who can only be known in relationship.*
>
> We should not be surprised to find that attributes which we sometimes associate primarily with purity and judgment are used to underscore God's mercy and compassion. (italics added)

Kutz then refers to Hosea 11:8–9 and reasons, "The question is[:] how will you and I respond to the invitation of such a God—a God who reminds us that he will bring all of his character to bear on our behalf? As the infinite God of the universe he is not obligated to do this. It is an invitation of supreme magnitude."[3]

Yes, God is merciful; mercy conveys the idea that God is not obligated to act compassionately on our behalf. Certainly, God is righteous and will judge sin and injustice. If we are honest with ourselves, we would have it no other way. The only caveat is that we often wish we were God so that we could pass judgment ourselves on those who provoke us and do wrong to us and those close to us—after all, we're number one. However, the one who is truly number one is merciful toward us:

> The LORD, the LORD, a God merciful and gracious, slow to anger, and abounding in steadfast love and faithfulness, keeping steadfast love for thousands, forgiving iniquity and transgression and sin, but who will by no means clear the guilty, visiting the iniquity of the fathers on the children and the children's children, to the third and the fourth generation. (Exod 34:6–7)

God is not obligated to treat us mercifully, but he does. This is one of the reasons why he is truly number one. We see the core of his being revealed in Jesus, who not only declared that those who are merciful toward others are truly blessed (Matt 5:7), but who also lived it out to the very end, even while providing judgment on sin in himself on the cross. There he cries out to his Father regarding those responsible for his crucifixion: "Father, forgive them, for they know not what they do" (Luke 23:34).

If this is how God treats us—and we are all responsible in one way or another for Jesus' suffering and death, how can we not extend his mercy to those around us, especially those who appear to be in greatest need? More than a paradox, it is a contradiction in terms to act without mercy and claim Christ. May we be logically and existentially consistent and pour out mercy as the recipients of God's compassion of unfathomable extravagance.

3. Kutz, "Torah Scroll Dedication."

Cultural Reflection: Who Locked Up Mercy and Threw Away the Key?

It's not easy to find mercy in our society today. In reflecting upon personal examples of mercy, I was hard-pressed to find them. It's almost as if someone locked up mercy and threw away the key.

Take driving down the highway. We can feel so easily slighted by other drivers, as we are locked up behind metal and glass in our cars, SUVs, and trucks. Try using your turn signal to change lanes. Some drivers will speed up so that you can't merge, while others will cut you off from entering the freeway, or ride your bumper to save their gas when you do merge. They (we?) feel entitled to the mercy of others, and hoard it as if it's in short supply.

One would assume it would be even more difficult to find mercy in a prison, where people are locked up, hand-cuffed, and sometimes put in chains. But God's mercy is not chained and can show up anywhere, even behind bars.

Steve is a chaplain in a medium-security prison. He's required by law to provide support for all faith communities represented there, including help with their services. So, not only does Steve support Christians in worship, but also he supports the religious expression of Jews, Muslims, Buddhists, Native Americans, Wiccans, and a variety of other groups. It's not easy for Steve, as he is a fundamentalist-evangelical Christian. But he does so with great care and love, knowing how important it is to these incarcerated persons that they express themselves freely in one of the few areas where the prison system does not lock them up—their souls.

In my encounters with Steve, I have found him to become all things to all people. Yet in doing so, he has become more fully like Jesus Christ. By being merciful toward those behind bars, he has become increasingly a beneficiary of God's mercy, too. Steve realizes that our hearts are really locked from the inside and that God desires to set us free. By being merciful, he has experienced increasingly God's mercy revealed in Jesus. Steve knows full well you can never outdo or out-mercy God. As Matthew 5:7 declares, we will receive God's mercy when we operate mercifully toward others. I myself come away from our visits more fully alive to the good news, as Steve speaks so graciously and affirmatively. There's even a bit more bounce in my step as I walk about freely in society, a little less encumbered by my own merciless ambition's ball and chain.

One should not think that Steve is but a carefree spirit, a maverick who throws the law books to the wind and springs people from jail. He goes according to the script that aims to protect the inmates, the security guards, and other staff. He does not allow those entrusted to his spiritual care to get control of him either, as some are always looking for an angle or inroad into how to manipulate him and work the system.

There are dangers, as fights break out, or those incarcerated may even threaten to hurt Steve or those close to him. Once, during a phone conversation, he told me in passing that he barely avoided being punched on three separate occasions that day. Moreover, given their lack of freedoms, some get explosive if they feel their spiritual self-expression is not honored. While not intimidated, Steve wants to make sure their human dignity is affirmed and their desired spiritual expression is honored, when almost everything else has been taken away from them.

While Steve does not proselytize, still many inmates of other paths come to believe in Jesus through his thoughtful and caring regard for supporting their own faith expression. Some have noted how struck they are by his humble and loving service. While he does not serve this captive audience in some bait-and-switch manner, still humility has a way of speaking for itself. Perhaps these new believers in Jesus are drawn in part because humility and mercy are in short supply in a system that often humbles them mercilessly, reminding them daily in various ways that they are guilty as charged. And what then about the rest of us who are free to drive down the road? If we can't operate mercifully toward other drivers, but demand mercy from them, maybe the authorities should take away our keys.

Questions

1. What connection might there be between the beatitude on mercy and the beatitudes on righteousness (Matt 5:6) and purity (Matt 5:8) that precede it and follow it? Do you immediately think of people who are righteous as merciful? What connection might there be between those who embody mercy and the pure of heart?

2. In view of the Bible, do you think someone who is not merciful can be righteous, just, and pure of heart?

3. Consider people in your own experience whom you would deem to be merciful. How does their demonstration of mercy fit with the biblical discussion of mercy set forth here, as well as the example of Steve, the prison chaplain?

4. Is mercy a rare "commodity" or scarce "jewel" in society today, in your estimation? Please give some examples in support of why you think mercy is either plentiful or scarce?

5. In your estimation, do you think there is a connection between experiencing mercy and extending mercy? In other words, do you think that it is hard to extend mercy if we do not believe God and others have been merciful to us?

6. If mercy is viewed as a commodity, it is easy to think that we need to keep it in a safe so we do not lose it, especially if it is in short supply. If, however, mercy is like a muscle, isn't it the case that if we use it, it will grow? What do you think? What difference might it make in your experience if you were to consider how to extend mercy to others more regularly? How might your own experience of comprehending God's mercy toward you change or grow?

7. In view of Jesus calling his disciples to him (they did not call themselves), and in view of realizing our spiritual need for God as the first sign of blessedness (Matt 5:3), how might you relate divine mercy to the whole of your understanding of discipleship?

7

"Blessed Are the Pure in Heart"
—Not the Double-minded
and Those with Cloudy Vision

Biblical Meditation

I still remember a friend of my Mother asking her, "What has happened to Paul?" I was a high school student at the time; she said that my eyes had become dark. I had cloudy vision. My eyes were a reflection of the conflicted state of my soul during that troubling season in my life. Perhaps you have heard the expression, "The eye is the window to the soul." Jesus said as much, as have some scientists.

In Matthew 6, Jesus declares,

> The eye is the lamp of the body. So, if your eye is healthy, your whole body will be full of light, but if your eye is bad, your whole body will be full of darkness. If then the light in you is darkness, how great is the darkness! No one can serve two masters, for either he will hate the one and love the other, or he will be devoted to the one

and despise the other. You cannot serve God and money (Matt 6:22–24).

A *Daily Mail* article titled "Scientists Discover That Eyes Really Are 'the Window to the Soul'" reports of scientists at Oreobro University in Sweden claiming that

> Those with densely packed crypts [in this case crypts are threads that radiate from the pupil, not places where you bury the dead!] are more warmhearted, tender, trusting, and likely to sympathise with others. In comparison, those with more contraction furrows were more neurotic, impulsive and likely to give way to cravings.
>
> The researchers argued that eye structure and personality could be linked because the genes responsible for the development of the iris also play a role in shaping part of the frontal lobe of the brain, which influences personality . . . .
>
> The results will be published in the *American Journal of Biological Psychology*. "Our results suggest people with different iris features tend to develop along different personality lines," said Matt Larsson, a behavioural scientist who led the study at Orebro University.[1]

I do not claim that my high school experience and the scientific study are detailing the same phenomenon, but I do believe that my experience resonates with Jesus' claim in Matthew 6. Here in Matthew 6 Jesus is performing eye and heart surgery. He often performs it on me, just as he did then in my youth. I was double-minded, seeking to serve two masters—Jesus and Jim Morrison, the deceased rock star. Actually, according to my Mom, Morrison had replaced Jesus as my Lord. The substance of my being, including my limited financial resources (mammon), went to breaking on through to the other side where Morrison could be found. My Mom's friend could sense my double-minded ways, which reflected a conflicted, impure soul.

---

1. "Scientists Discover That Eyes Really Are 'the Window to the Soul,'" lines 3–23, 27–32.

I would not have seen God, given my polluted soul. Here I call to mind Matthew 5:8: "Blessed are the pure in heart, for they shall see God." Only those with an undivided mind and heart will truly see God. *The Expositor's Greek Testament* makes a connection between Matthew 6:22 and Matthew 5:8, too, when it reasons that it was Jesus'

> habit to insist on the connection between clear vision and moral simplicity; to teach that it is the single eye that is full of light (Matt 6:22). It is true that the pure shall have access to God's presence, but the truth to be insisted on in connection with this Beatitude is that through purity, singleness of mind, they are qualified for seeing, knowing, truly conceiving God and all that relates to the moral universe. It is the pure in heart who are able to see and say that "truly God is good" (Ps 73:1) and rightly to interpret the whole phenomena of life in relation to Providence. They shall see, says Jesus casting His thought into eschatological form, but He means the pure are the men who see; the double-minded, the two-souled (*dipsuchos*, Jas 1:8) man, is blind.[2]

How does Matthew 5:8 fit within the overall context of the Beatitudes? Here is my take. Those who receive God's mercy (Matt 5:7) become pure in heart. Think of Isaiah, who when he sees God cries out in despair (Isa 6:5). Yet God does not destroy him, but mercifully reaches out and cleanses Isaiah and calls him to serve him in purity. As a result, Isaiah can see God all the more clearly and serve him all the more truly. In the Bible, purity of heart is connected to clear sight and clean lips (Isa 6:5–7). The pure of heart, sight, and lips become bearers of glad tidings of peace and joy.[3] The spiritually pure are not double-hearted or minded (Matt

---

2. Bruce, *The Expositor's Greek New Testament*, 99.

3. In Isaiah 6, we find that Isaiah is given a message of severe judgment (Isa 6:8–13); however, the word of judgment gives way to hope bound up with the messianic promise and hope for the faithful remnant (Isa 6:13); one must also account for the eschatological promise of blessing and shalom that is found in later chapters in Isaiah (e.g., Isa 60).

5:8), but calm of spirit and at peace. They are agents of God's peace (Matt 5:9), and are persecuted as a result (Matt 5:10).

Purity of heart is obviously important to Jesus. As seen in Matthew's Gospel, Jesus frames spirituality as centered in the heart (e.g., see Jesus' discussion of anger and lust in Matt 5:21–30; see also 15:1–20). Purity of heart is not an isolated phenomenon in Scripture. Further to what was noted above in Isaiah 6:5–7, one sees a fundamental connection between purity of heart and eye and mouth. Purity also involves innocence of hands. Those who are pure of heart are not violent. They do not shed innocent blood. They are peacemakers (Prov 6:16–19; Ps 24:3–6). They pursue righteousness and flee youthful passions (2 Tim 2:22). They are obedient to the truth, which involves sincere brotherly love (1 Pet 1:22). Indeed, those who are pure of heart are pure in other ways.

The pure of heart will truly see God. They will understand God's ways. They will experience the beatific vision—the complete and direct self-communication of God to them—when they see God face to face through the mediation of Jesus' countenance. It is worth noting here that, as with mercy, there is a sense of dynamism. Only those who experience God's mercy can be merciful, and in turn will be recipients of greater depths of mercy (Matt 5:7). Those who experience Christ for how pure he truly is will grow in purity. As they grow in purity, they will see God all the more clearly. The disciples would come to realize that their own purity of heart was bound up with seeing Christ, holding to his word, and following in his footsteps. We, too, are transformed, as we gaze upon him through his Word in the community of his disciples in the world (1 Pet 1:8; 1 John 3:1–3).

I have gotten glimpses of Jesus' purity over the years. The vision of him is purifying, as it exposes my double-mindedness. I may not be drawn to Jim Morrison as a rock god anymore (though I enjoy listening to his band's music), but I still get easily distracted by other deities of various kinds, including mammon. As a result, my vision becomes clouded and darkened. It reminds me of Jesus' discussion of parables in Matthew 13, where the Lord quotes from Isaiah 6. Here in Matthew 13, Jesus speaks of the deceitfulness of riches that choke the word, making it unfruitful: "As for what was sown among thorns, this is the one who hears the word, but the cares of the world and the deceitfulness of riches choke the word, and it proves unfruitful" (Matt 13:22). The parables reveal God's judgment on those who are hardened of heart and who do not see or listen to God's revelation in Jesus (Matt 13:10–17). They are double-minded with cloudy vision.

I want to be one who sees God and who listens to God, as revealed in Jesus. Those who do so are truly blessed, even more so than the prophets of old like Isaiah. As Jesus said to his disciples, "But blessed are your eyes, for they see, and your ears, for they hear. For truly, I say to you, many prophets and righteous people longed to see what you see, and did not see it, and to hear what you hear, and did not hear it" (Matt 13:16–17). I don't want to miss out on seeing Jesus because of looking this way and that, as some double-minded person with cloudy vision.

The Lord who called his disciples to him for this Sermon on the Mount calls us to himself today. Are we listening to his word and obeying him? Are we gazing solely on him?

May our heart's passion and drive be that of David, the man after God's own heart, who exclaimed, "One thing have I asked of the LORD, that will I seek after: that I may dwell in the house of the LORD all the days of my life, to gaze upon the beauty of the LORD and to inquire in his temple" (Ps 27:4).

After my high school years, I came across Keith Green, a modern-day David, whose song "O Lord, You're Beautiful" reflects a heart that is single-minded and whose vision is clear. At that time, I found his passion to break on through to Jesus far more compelling than Morrison's drive to break on through to the other side. I long for such single-minded devotion and clear vision today.

In the end, would you like to see God? Are you single-mindedly pursuing him now? Is your vision clear? Or like me, do you need eye and heart surgery again and again? "Blessed are the pure in heart, for they shall see God" (Matt 5:8).

Cultural Reflection: How Can We Become Pure of Heart If We Are Blind to Our Need for God and Others?

My friend Phil is blind. But his blindness does not keep him from seeing God's will for him. God has recently given him a new outlook or perspective on the Christian life. While Phil is a very hardworking, resilient, and creative business leader, he has come to realize he needs others' help more than most because of his blindness. He further realizes his need for God and fellow Christians.

Phil's account reminds me of the very first of the beatitudes in Matthew's Gospel, which highlights our desperate need for God in Jesus (Matt 5:3). Phil not only senses his physical need for help because of his physical blindness, but also his spiritual need for God. He is poor in spirit (Matt 5:3). How well do we see our need for God? Those who recognize their spiritual poverty are blessed (5:3). So, when we come to Matthew 5:8 on purity of heart, we need to recognize that we cannot conjure up purity, or perfect ourselves in holiness. We need God to cleanse our hearts if we are going to be pure in heart and see God (Matt 5:8). In Psalm 51:10, the psalmist cries out to God to create in him a clean heart. First John 1:9 exhorts us to confess our sins to God so that we will be made pure.

Phil perceives that apart from God and others it is hard to grow in holiness or purity of heart. We cannot go it alone. While only those who are pure in heart will see God, we can only become pure in heart with the communal aid and encouragement of God's Spirit and his people. In addition to asking God for forgiveness, we are to confess our sins to one another so that we can be healed (Jas 5:16).

All too often we are deceived into thinking that spiritual formation involving purification is solely an individual responsibility—that we have to go it alone. Nothing could be further from the truth. In fact, pride blinds us to our need and shoves us down so that we fall in the darkness. In contrast, purity of heart, which helps us see God and the path to godliness, involves confession of sin to God and his people.

One of the striking qualities of Phil's perception is how well he sees through his other senses. While he cannot see people's facial expressions, he can sense aspects of their emotional state by listening to them breathe. He sees through sound, as well as through his other senses. He is often far more aware of his surroundings through his other senses than we are because he's attentive to running into people, walls, and objects since he can't count on seeing them.

How well are we aware of our surroundings, our need for mercy and reconciliation through confession? In a similar manner, how well are we aware of the immediate surroundings of Matthew 5:8? Mercy precedes purity of heart (5:7) and peace-making follows it (5:9).

Just as Phil relies on the mercy of others to get around at times, so he is aware of the need for peace-making. If people are not merciful toward one another, they will run into each other. We need to become aware of how we run into each other and over one another so that we can alter our course and run together.

It's no coincidence that, as a Japanese man whose parents lived in an internment camp during World War II, prior to his birth, Phil has made a professional career as a diversity consultant and trainer. He understands the importance of seeing one another more clearly, being merciful and reconciled to each other, and making transformative peace.

Before Phil's birth, his family moved from the internment camp to a farm elsewhere in the States. Given that so many men went overseas to fight the Germans and Japanese during WWII, his father was given the task of farming stateside. Just as his parents had been forcibly moved about since Pearl Harbor, so Phil was forcibly delivered into this world. The night he was born, the doctor said, "I don't work on Japs after midnight." So, the doctor used forceps to pull Phil out of his mother's womb before midnight and before Phil was ready to be born.

Just like Pearl Harbor and Hiroshima, internment camps, and forced premature deliveries, we keep forcing ourselves on one another rather than operating mercifully. Phil's blindness helps him to see far more clearly his need for spiritual help, and our own. How clear is your spiritual vision? We need to confess our sins to God and one another to be healed and become pure of heart. Let's lead one another by the hand.

Questions

1. Having read the biblical meditation on Matthew 5:8 and this cultural reflection, you find that much is made of purity of heart not being an isolated phenomenon. In the Bible, purity of heart is not isolated from our eyes, mouth, and hands. Furthermore, it is not isolated from God and others: we need God and others to help us grow in purity. Moreover, it is not isolated from the beatitudes that precede it and follow it, such as being merciful (Matt 5:7) and making peace (Matt 5:9). How often do you view the various dimensions of life as isolated from one another? How does it affect your spirituality, including purity of heart?

2. How important are the objects of our gaze to becoming pure of heart or, from the opposite angle, double-minded and cloudy in vision? Please offer an example or two of how what you gaze upon purifies or fractures and clouds your spiritual vision.

3. Being single-minded is not the same thing as having tunnel vision, where we fail to see those around us or how everything is connected. How do you make sense of the difference between single-mindedness and tunnel vision, while growing in the former and safeguarding against the latter?

4. How does confession of sin to God lead to purification? (1 John 1:9) How might confession of sin to someone else aid in one's purification process? (Jas 5:16) Have you ever confessed your sins to someone as a result of reading James 5:16?

Why or why not? If you have, what did you experience as a result? How do you discern who is safe to confess to? Is there ever a danger that someone can take the place of God, who alone can cleanse us from sin? If we only confess to God and not others, what might that suggest about our lives?

5. How important is receiving mercy from others and offering mercy to others (Matt 5:7) to becoming pure of heart? How important is the pursuit of purity of heart to being a peacemaker? (Matt 5:9).

8

"Blessed Are the Peacemakers" —Not the Cheesemakers

Biblical Meditation

Matthew 5:9 reads, "Blessed are the peacemakers, for they shall be called sons of God." This verse is one of the most quoted lines of the Beatitudes, but that does not mean it is the best understood. In fact, it has been misprinted, as in the second edition of the Geneva Bible. There it reads, "Blessed are the placemakers." Monty Python took the liberty of people in the crowd mishearing Jesus' words for a few good laughs in *Life of Brian*—"Blessed are the cheesemakers."[1]

The problem goes beyond misprinting or mishearing the statement. Perhaps the Romans listening in or reading Jesus' words thought he had Rome's peace—the *Pax Romana*—in mind. After all, as Douglas R. A. Hare notes, Jesus uttered these words during the *Pax Romana*, when Rome had established peace and brought to an end small wars between various peoples, ended pirating, and diminished greatly highway banditry. However, its forces could not

---

1. *Monty Python's Life of Brian*. To view this classic movie scene, refer to the following website: https://www.youtube.com/watch?v=slbMe-aTY1A&app=desktop.

establish the Shalom that the Jewish Scriptures envision: "harmonious cooperation aimed at the welfare of all."[2] Going further, Augustus's reforms, known as the Roman peace, lasted a few hundred years and achieved a great deal for the Roman Empire politically, economically, and socially. Augustus sought to establish Rome as a capital for the entire world and instructed the Romans to view their destiny as that of all humanity. Caesar and the "heavenly city" of his subjects brought order and tranquility to the world in chaos through the Roman peace.[3]

I always get a bit fearful when someone or some group takes it upon themselves to establish peace, especially by violent and oppressive force, like the Romans did. Rome created incredible turmoil to bring about its envisioned messianic peace. Jesus did not have in mind the *Pax Romana* (peace of Rome) but the *Pax Christi*, which is the eschatological fulfillment of the Hebrew Scriptures' emphasis on Shalom. As Jürgen Moltmann claims, Jesus confronts the Roman rule of retribution by way of redemption, grace, and the cross.[4]

Perhaps the Zealots understood Jesus' words to entail the removal of the *Pax Romana*—by violent force.[5] After all, Jesus claimed to be the Son of Man, the long-awaited Messiah or Christ. And yet, why would he establish his rule by way of the cross, and why would he take a tax collector like Matthew—the author of this Gospel—into his inner circle, along with Simon the Zealot? Tax collectors were traitors among the Jewish people who did the bidding of Rome in collecting taxes and making a great profit in the process at the expense of their countrymen. While Matthew left his tax-collector booth behind (Luke 5:27–28), he did not become a Zealot, but a disciple of Jesus, which involves an alternative or counter-kingdom order to that envisaged by Romans or Zealots.

---

2. Hare, *Matthew*, 42.

3. Oakesmith, *The Religion of Plutarch*, 79–80.

4. See Moltmann, *The Crucified God*, 136–45.

5. See Kohler, "Zealots," paragraph 11.

Jesus' view of peace does not resonate well with either Roman or Zealot peace.[6]

It is not just the Romans, Zealots, or tax collectors that can miss what Jesus is trying to say. All of us can miss it. All too often, we function like the characters in the Monty Python movie noted earlier. We may not mishear Jesus to say, "Blessed are the cheesemakers." Rather, we might be like some of the others in the crowd who for whatever reason fail to apply what Jesus says. Instead, we start fighting, rather than make peace with one another, or depart for a stoning, like the woman (Brian's mother) who finds a stoning more entertaining or meaningful than listening to Jesus. Some of us might operate like the movie's religious leader in the crowd who says we should not take cheese making literally ("cheese making" can refer to any dairy manufacturer). Those of us who follow this religious leader's example do the same thing with peacemaking—we think Jesus wants for us to take "peacemaking" figuratively.

But Jesus *does* want us to take his words literally. We are to be peacemakers. While we do not initiate peace with God—since God must be (and is) the one who initiates and reconciles us to himself, we are to respond affirmatively and be reconciled to God.[7] Following from being reconciled to God, we are to initiate and seek peace with one another. Indeed, peace with God that is established by God's rule in our lives through the *Pax Christi* (peace of

6. See Jesus' words later in this very chapter—Matthew 5:38–49; note also that when given the opportunity to resist by force, Jesus rebukes Peter for cutting off his would-be captor's ear with a sword, heals the ear, and goes willingly with his would-be captors, ever in full control of all the proceedings (Luke 22:47–53; John 18:1–11). Jesus' peace does not resonate with tax-collector peace either; for Jesus tells his followers not simply to love those who love them, which even the tax collectors do, but also to love their enemies (Matt 5:46).

7. Here I call to mind 2 Corinthians 5:18–21: "All this is from God, who through Christ *reconciled us to himself* and gave us the ministry of reconciliation; that is, *in Christ God was reconciling the world to himself*, not counting their trespasses against them, and entrusting to us the message of reconciliation. Therefore, we are ambassadors for Christ, God making his appeal through us. We implore you on behalf of Christ, *be reconciled to God*. For our sake he made him to be sin who knew no sin, so that in him we might become the righteousness of God" (italics added).

Christ) entails the effort to be at peace with our fellow humans. We must never separate reconciliation with God from reconciliation with neighbor. Matthew's Gospel emphasizes both aspects, as does Luke's Gospel. In the latter Gospel, the chief tax collector Zacchaeus makes peace with others by making amends for his wrongs against them, showing that salvation has come to his house and that he is a "son of Abraham" (Luke 19:1–10).[8] Peacemaking entails more than simply avoiding war with others or being "peaceful." It involves *making* peace with people.[9]

There is nothing passive about making peace. It is hard, active work. It is God's ongoing activity, as he reconciles the world to himself through his Son. God truly views those who make peace as his sons and children, as we make peace (Matthew 5:9 and 5:44–45 make a connection between "eschatological sonship and peacemaking").[10] Children copy what their parents do.

Think of Isaiah, who was truly a son of Abraham. As such, he was a bearer of God's tidings of peace. In the previous chapter titled "'Blessed are the Pure in Heart'—Not the Double-minded and Those with Cloudy Vision," I referred to Isaiah as one who became a bearer of God's good news of peace and joy, when God cleansed him (Isa 6). He exhorted the people in his day to be reconciled to God. The book of Isaiah declares, "How beautiful upon the mountains are the feet of him who brings good news, who publishes peace, who brings good news of happiness, who publishes salvation, who says to Zion, 'Your God reigns'" (Isa 52:7; cf. Rom 10:15). The tragic irony is that the rulers and people ultimately rejected Isaiah's message and him. Tradition tells us that he

8. Further to Jesus' claim that Zacchaeus is a son of Abraham, John the Baptist and Jesus maintained that those who belong to Abraham by repentance and faith in God's reconciling, peacemaking activity through the Messiah, God's Son Jesus, belong to God (Matt 3:9; John 8:39–47). Zacchaeus is a true child of Abraham, for he has repented of his past life and believed in Jesus, who has come to seek and save the lost (Luke 19:10).

9. See Davies and Allison, *Matthew*, 457.

10. Ibid., 459. They also write, "What is hoped for and symbolized by the notion of eschatological sonship is twofold—(1) a degree of intimacy with God heretofore not experienced and (2) a likeness to him (cf. 5.48)." (Ibid., 549).

was sawn in two (Heb 11:37) by the order of Manasseh king of Judah.[11] Like father, like son—Isaiah is a peacemaker, just like God. Or to put it in other terms: like God's Messiah, like his prophets. It is no coincidence that in the very next beatitude Jesus declares that those who are persecuted for righteousness' sake are blessed—the kingdom of heaven belongs to them. Like Isaiah and other prophets of old, Jesus' peacemaking followers bear witness to Jesus, the prince of peace. They are persecuted for it (Matt 5:10–12).

Not everything that passes for peace functions as a form of God's peace. God's peace involves God's reign, as Isaiah 52:7 referenced above makes clear. Not everyone wants God's reign. God's peace revealed in Jesus disturbs unjust tranquility. The prophets of old who foreshadowed Jesus also disturbed unjust tranquility. Further to what was said above, God's righteous prophets of old told the rulers of Israel and Judah that calamity would befall them for their unjust dealings. There would be no peace no matter how much the rulers of the people wished or declared it because they did not obey God by following his law, which involved justice for the people and the land. The rulers did not like hearing the message of the prophets that called them to repent and enter into God's kingdom Shalom. As a result, those in power persecuted the godly prophets like Isaiah and Jeremiah. Like them, we will be persecuted for calling for God's peace to replace an unjust peace.

In closing, it is important to note that opposition and persecution are not always overt. Opposition can take the form of moderation—moderates often prefer order to justice.[12] Just think of Martin Luther King Jr.'s situation. King was jailed for confronting unjust laws of segregation with justice. He was imprisoned for disturbing the peace—an unjust peace. The preachers of Birmingham confronted him for it. We will close with a portion of his prophetic rejoinder in his "Letter from a Birmingham Jail" written in 1963:

11. See Hirsch, Cheyne, Singer, and Broydé, "Isaiah," paragraph 7.

12. I am not referring to political moderates as such, but to those who simply seek to maintain a sense of equilibrium between (seemingly) opposing schemes no matter the cost.

I must make two honest confessions to you, my Christian and Jewish brothers. First, I must confess that over the last few years I have been gravely disappointed with the white moderate. I have almost reached the regrettable conclusion that the Negro's great stumbling block in his stride toward freedom is not the White Citizen's Counciler or the Ku Klux Klanner, but the white moderate who is more devoted to "order" than to justice; who prefers a negative peace which is the absence of tension to a positive peace which is the presence of justice; who constantly says: "I agree with you in the goal you seek, but I can't agree with your methods of direct action"; who paternalistically feels he can set the timetable for another man's freedom; who lives by the myth of time and who constantly advised the Negro to wait for a "more convenient season." Shallow understanding from people of good will is more frustrating than absolute misunderstanding from people of ill will. Lukewarm acceptance is much more bewildering than outright rejection.[13]

Many of us may promote injustice by preferring a negative peace, which is the absence of tension. But King knew that justice often requires tension: "I am not afraid of the word 'tension.' I have earnestly worked and preached against violent tension, but there is a type of constructive nonviolent tension that is necessary for growth."[14] Perhaps this is the means through which we can harmonize Jesus' blessing the peacemakers and his bringing a sword of some kind (Matt 10:34)? Regardless, we must not harmonize injustice with peace.

Do we avoid tension for the sake of order, even if it puts justice on hold? There's something very cheesy about such peace. Those who avoid tension for the sake of order apart from justice are not agents of peace. Peace with God involves the just ordering of our relationships, whereby we love God even as we love our neighbors as ourselves (Mark 12:30–31). Jesus would have us take his words about peace quite literally.

13. In *A Testament of Hope,* 295.
14. Ibid., 291.

Cultural Reflection: How Can We Be Peacemakers If We Are Pugnacious, or Too Nice?

It's very hard to be a peacemaker if one is not a peaceful person. It's also very hard to be a peacemaker if one is not able to see clearly one's own part in a conflict, as well as others' roles. Moreover, it's very hard to make peace if one is simply nice, or simply trying to keep the peace.

David is a friend of mine from Uganda. He's a peaceful person. He calms me down just by my visiting with him—I should visit with him more often. David often has a keen awareness of various parties' roles in a conflict, including his own. According to David, one of his problems as a Ugandan is that he's too nice. He maintains that he and many of his fellow Ugandans want to get along and keep the peace. Keeping the peace, though, is not the same thing as making peace. Matthew 5:9 does not state that peace*keepers* are blessed, but rather peace*makers*. People can keep an unjust peace, a point that Dr. King brought home in his "Letter from a Birmingham Jail." Making peace is a different matter altogether, especially in the case of the Sermon on the Mount, which entails Jesus' envisioned kingdom shalom.

Still, one can appreciate the desire simply to get along and keep the peace, especially if one was raised in a war-torn region like Uganda. David barely escaped being killed on several occasions as a youth in the aftermath following Idi Amin's reign of terror. Now a seasoned and mature Christian leader who is highly regarded by Christian missionaries and Ugandan nationals, he finds himself at a crossroads in a very different kind of conflict.

David has observed how often it's the case that the missionaries and Ugandans get along quite well until the Ugandan Christians rise to a certain level of maturity and desire to take on more leadership responsibilities. David loves both groups deeply, and is indebted to both as a home-grown leader, who was raised by the Ugandan people and mentored by missionaries.

David feels a deep sense of "Ubuntu" (a profound, abiding interconnection) with both parties in the conflict. And so, it pains him to share that from his perspective the missionaries have often operated in a paternalistic manner and the Ugandans, himself included, have not been forthright until matters get out of hand. They have been too nice much of the time and the missionaries have been controlling much of the time.

I expect that no matter how peaceful and peaceable David is, he is going to experience pushback the more he proceeds down the path of trying to make peace with his fellow Christian brothers and sisters from the West and from Uganda. He has already experienced some level of pushback when he raises these matters. While it's not persecution as such, he can take comfort from the fact that the very next (and last) beatitude that follows 5:9 is 5:10: Jesus blesses those who are persecuted for righteousness' sake (5:10). Dr. King did not fare too well with White moderates, Aryan Supremacists, or Black Nationalists, and yet his whole aim was to pursue a just peace that would build beloved community involving people of all backgrounds.

David is realizing that while it's never good to be *pugnacious*, it's always very good to be *tenacious* in the pursuit of peace. It won't be easy. After all, the tensions go way back in history.[15] The West carved up most of Africa, with Uganda falling to Britain. Faced with internal tensions brewing, Britain sought to quell the turmoil by giving nominal rule over the whole of Uganda to one tribal leader only to increase strife in other regions. Those who don't understand history tend to repeat it, and the history of the conflict is very long with various streams or tributaries, like the river Nile.

As with these global conflicts, our own personal conflicts have long and complex histories. While not all cats are gray, and some parties are more guilty than others, we need to come to terms with our own roles in conflicts—whether as aggressors, reactors, or pacifiers. As David has realized, we all need to be tenacious, not pugnacious or submissive in the pursuit of Jesus' just kingdom

---

15. Harmon, *Central and East Africa*, 94.

peace. It's worth the effort, for God calls righteous peacemakers his children and those to whom his kingdom belongs (Matt 5:9–10).

Questions

1. Would you agree that there is a difference between peacekeeping and peacemaking? Why or why not? If you do see a difference, how would you articulate it?

2. Some people seek to enforce peace, which can be a form of pugnaciousness. The Roman peace (*Pax Romana*) was a form of such enforcement. What would be a similar example today? How so?

3. Further to the last set of questions, enforcing peace does not address the heart issue. What is distinctive about Jesus as the Prince of Peace as he enters our lives? How does he bring about peace? What might you and I learn from his example and how might we live in the Spirit of God and operate like Jesus?

4. David's story brings to mind how power dynamics must be accounted for in Christian ministry and missions, including when cultivating and making peace. David is trying to address the power dynamics and different ways the Western missionaries and Ugandan national leaders deal with conflict. How might you become more attentive to power dynamics in a given conflict as well as how different groups respond to conflict—paternalistically, passively . . . ? How might you address them?

5. David realized that being nice can stand in the way of being reconciled. Are there situations in your own life experience where you or others are nice, but it stands in the way of making peace? How might you or others in your midst proceed to be loving and caring with the aim of pursuing reconciliation, and not resorting simply to being nice?

6. In the biblical exposition of Matthew 5:9, consideration was given to Zealots and tax collectors. Jesus' inner circle of disciples included people who would otherwise be at odds or at war with one another. In addition to Simon the Zealot and Matthew the tax collector, his most intimate inner circle included the Sons of Thunder, James and John (Mark 3:17), whom he rebuked for their harsh reaction to the Samaritans' response to Jesus. (Luke 9:54–55; some manuscripts add to Luke 9:55–56: "You do not know what manner of spirit you are of; . . . for the Son of Man came not to destroy people's lives but to save them.") It is far easier to keep or make peace with people who are already inclined toward one another in various ways, and with those who are generally gentle and agreeable. But Jesus' peacemaking efforts go in a different direction, as he unites warring and warlike people, loving even his own enemies, just like his Father in heaven (Matt 5:44–45). What might it look like if we envisioned church along such reconciling lines, bringing together diverse and even warring and warlike peoples? How might it bear on our witness as salt and light in society? (Matt 5:13–16).

7. As stated in the biblical reflection, it is no coincidence that the beatitude immediately following "peace making" (5:9) is about being persecuted for righteousness (Matt 5:10). Not all forms of peacekeeping and peacemaking are righteous, but those that are may lead to the peacemaker being persecuted. Jesus forewarned his disciples to be prepared for persecution for making peace in his name. Just as David is receiving pushback for seeking to make peace among Jesus' people called to proclaim his kingdom in Uganda, you may experience pushback as well in your various missional contexts with believers and those who do not yet know Jesus. But as will be made clear from the final beatitude and the ensuing discussion (Matt 5:10–16), those who shrink back from the pursuit of making peace cannot be salt and light. How will you discern if your peacemaking efforts are righteous? And how might Jesus' encouragement that those who make peace

in a righteous manner are children of the Father and that the kingdom of God belongs to them? (Matt 5:9–10).

9

"Blessed Are Those Who Are Persecuted for Righteousness' Sake"
—Not Tax Evasion

Biblical Meditation

No doubt, the apostle Peter had Jesus' words recorded in Matthew in mind when he encouraged and exhorted Christians to suffer for *righteousness'* sake, and not for murder, thievery, evil, meddling—and no doubt deception like tax evasion:

> Beloved, do not be surprised at the fiery trial when it comes upon you to test you, as though something strange were happening to you. But rejoice insofar as you share Christ's sufferings, that you may also rejoice and be glad when his glory is revealed. If you are insulted for the name of Christ, you are blessed, because the Spirit of glory and of God rests upon you. But let none of you suffer as a murderer or a thief or an evildoer or as a meddler. Yet if anyone suffers as a Christian, let him not be ashamed, but let him glorify God in that name. (1 Pet 4:12–16; for the fuller context of Peter's development of this theme, see 1 Pet 3:8–22 and 1 Pet 4:12–19)

Indeed, it sounds like he is alluding to "Blessed are those who are persecuted for righteousness' sake, for theirs is the kingdom of heaven" (Matt 5:10).

Peter's words were timely given that his audience was facing various trials. His words are also timely today given that many Christians in the States could be taken by surprise when they suffer persecution. We should not be surprised when we suffer judgment for doing evil. Nor should we be surprised as Christians when we suffer persecution for living in keeping with Jesus' righteousness. Someone might ask, "How can that be? Don't we belong to the King of kings?" While we do belong to the King of kings, whose kingdom will last forever, the present age that is passing away fights against the expansion of Jesus' kingdom reign. Jesus' kingdom (which is identified with God's kingdom or the kingdom of heaven) has been established, but it has not yet been realized in full. So, we will experience persecution until his glorious return, as Jesus and Peter inform us.

As noted above, God's kingdom has been established, but it has not yet been realized in full. George Eldon Ladd and others have written at length on the "now" and "not yet" dimensions of the kingdom.[1] We find this twofold teaching on the kingdom being present and future in Jesus' Beatitudes. The beatitudes recorded in verses 3 and 10 indicate that Jesus' true disciples belong to his kingdom presently. Those who are poor in spirit and persecuted for righteousness' sake are blessed because "theirs *is* the kingdom of heaven" (Matt 5:3, 10; italics added).

Verses 3 and 10 serve as bookends (they function as a literary envelope known as an "inclusio"),[2] positioning all the other beatitudes that are set forth in between under one heading—reflections and rewards of the kingdom. Those who belong to Jesus' kingdom as his disciples reflect the character of the King and his kingdom. All of the beatitudes note the distinctive traits of their discipleship, including poverty of spirit (verse 3) and persecution for righteous-

1. Ladd, *The Gospel of the Kingdom*, 24–51.

2. See D. A. Carson's distinctive handling of the inclusio or inclusion in the Beatitudes in *The Sermon on the Mount*, 9.

ness (verse 10). In addition to receiving Jesus' kingdom presently, they will also receive rewards for reflecting his character and that of his kingdom. This leads us to note the future dimension of Jesus' kingdom reality.

The beatitudes presented in verses 4–9 highlight the future dimension and rewards for those who belong to Jesus' kingdom: those who mourn now "*shall be* comforted" (verse 4; italics added throughout this paragraph); those who are meek "*shall* inherit the earth" (verse 5); those who hunger and thirst for righteousness "*shall be* satisfied" (verse 6); those who are merciful presently "*shall* receive mercy" (verse 7); those who are pure of heart "*shall* see God" (verse 8); and those who are peacemakers "*shall be* called" sons of God (verse 9).

It is important for those who are being persecuted to know that they belong to Jesus and his kingdom. Their belonging is not simply future; it is a present reality: "Blessed are those who are persecuted for righteousness' sake, for theirs *is* the kingdom of heaven" (Matt 5:10; italics added). Moreover, their sense of belonging takes on even greater significance because they belong to a holy order that extends all the way back to the prophets of old, like Isaiah and Jeremiah noted in the previous chapter. Jesus' followers should not doubt that they are suffering for a worthwhile cause. Jesus means to convey that like the prophets of old, they suffer for Jesus! As Jesus declares,

> Blessed are you when others revile you and persecute you and utter all kinds of evil against you falsely *on my account*. Rejoice and be glad, for your reward is great in heaven, *for so they persecuted the prophets who were before you*. (Matt 5:11–12; italics added)

No wonder Jesus exclaims that those who suffer for identifying with him should rejoice and be glad. They are in exceptionally good company as participants of his kingdom along with the prophets who suffered before them in bearing witness to God's reign, which culminates in Jesus. And yet, we often shrink back in fear today, when considering the possibility of experiencing persecution. While no one should seek persecution, it will seek us out as Christians. This is not paranoia; this is a providential fact bound up with pursuing Christ. Just as Jesus experiences persecution, so, too, do his followers. In addition to Matthew's Gospel's emphasis on identification with Jesus' suffering persecution, John, Paul, and Peter also make the connection. We have already accounted for Peter's statements in 1 Peter 3 and 4. John's Gospel records Jesus as saying that bound up with abiding in him is experiencing what he experiences. We will experience persecution, since servants are not above their masters (John 15:18–27). Paul informs us that everyone who wants to live a godly life in Christ Jesus will be persecuted, as he himself was persecuted (2 Tim 3:10–13). In fact, all the apostles were.

It is important that Jesus and the apostles forewarn us that we will undergo persecution as Jesus' followers. It is also important that Jesus informs us of how important it is that we do not shrink back and avoid identification with him. The verses immediately following that refer to salt and light are relevant here. We must not fail to shine the light of the good news of Jesus Christ in the world. We must also be careful not to avoid suffering for the faith. Light is a penetrating force, whereas salt is a preserving force. The world can never experience the good news of Jesus in its fullness if we refuse to penetrate the darkness and preserve the world from decay. Our witness, including our suffering persecution, is essential to the world coming to know the redemptive mercies of God revealed in Jesus.

If we shrink back from suffering for the faith as a preserving influence in the world, but rather hide or escape from the world, we lose our saltiness, as Paul Minear makes clear. According to Minear, salt was an essential component in the temple liturgy/worship in ancient times.[3] The priests salted the sacrifices. According to Jesus, persecution/suffering/sacrifice is a key characteristic trait of his followers. Jesus' disciples' saltiness and suffering for their faith were indissolubly one. When disciples avoid suffering for the gospel, they lose out on the gospel's power (saltiness).[4]

3. Minear, "The Salt of the Earth," 34.
4. Ibid., 36.

Not everyone seeks to evade paying taxes. But many if not all of us would rather evade suffering for the faith. Concern over tax evasion is relevant, especially during tax season with the April 15th deadline for filing income tax returns looming large. Even more so is concern over 'persecution evasion,' since persecution of Christians worldwide has been on the increase for some time. Christian martyrdom doubled in 2013.[5]

No one wants to suffer, except perhaps masochists. So, why would Christians endure persecution? To be identified with Jesus—the Lord of the kingdom—and the saints of old. Christians who experience persecution are in special company. We are also in special company when we identify with our brothers and sisters today who suffer for their faith. Just think of our Egyptian brothers who were martyred in dramatic fashion by ISIS.[6] ISIS warned the church: "We're coming to get you."[7] In the midst of such persecution and ominous threats, it is quite striking to read the following lines from Bishop Feloubes Fawzy whose nephew and four cousins were martyred: "I am happy for my relatives. They had faith in God. They had faith in Jesus Christ. And that is what matters. . . . They died for their faith. They died for Christianity."[8] According to *Christianity Today's* coverage,

> "The name of Jesus was the last word on their lips. And like the early church martyrs, they entrusted themselves to the one who would receive them soon after. That name, whispered in the last moments, was like the seal of their martyrdom," Catholic Bishop Antonios Aziz Mina of Giza said, following Pope Francis's message denouncing the killings.[9]

---

5. Newman, "Christian Martyrdom Doubled in 2013."

6. See the following news articles, BBC, "Islamic State: Egyptian Christians Held in Libya Killed," February 15, 2015 and Rashad, "Coptic Christian Village Mourns," March 8, 2015.

7. CNN, "ISIS Message to Christians," 00:05–00:45.

8. Rashad, "Coptic Christian Village Mourns," March 8, 2015.

9. Chui, "21 Christians Slain by ISIS," March 1, 2015.

Of course, we should denounce the killings, but not those who are persecuted for righteousness sake. Like the pope and bishops reported in this article, we should identify with them, and with all people who suffer persecution for their faith worldwide. Further to what Bishop Angaelos, the leader of the Coptic Orthodox Church in the United Kingdom, said, we all must call for the protection of rights of persecuted religious minorities of all faith traditions. As quoted in *The Huffington Post*, the bishop declared:

> This crime is not just a crime against Coptic Christians ... [i]t is a crime against humanity, and if there's anything we should stand for as human beings, first and foremost it's the sanctity of all human life.[10]

To be against Christ is to be against humanity, for he is the image of God *and* the image of the new humanity. Thus, we should pray and call for the deliverance of Christians *and* all persecuted religious minorities.[11]

And yet, what if God does not deliver us from persecution? While we should pray for deliverance, we should also pray for those who endure persecution that they would remain faithful to Christ in the midst of it. Years ago, a noted Christian theologian shared of how he informed a Romanian pastor that the church in America was praying for their deliverance from horrible persecution under a totalitarian regime. The pastor asked the theologian not to pray for the removal of persecution, but their resilience in the face of it. This pastor's perspective was strikingly different.

We might not be the kind of Christians who go to prison for tax evasion, but we may be the kind who evade paying the cost for our Christian faith. While grace is free, it is a costly grace, as Dietrich Bonhoeffer noted in *The Cost of Discipleship*.[12] It is by no

---

10. Kuruvilla, "Coptic Christian," February 21, 2015.

11. With this point in mind, see the following article I co-authored with John W. Morehead titled "Don't Be Indifferent to Religious Persecution. Make a Multi-Faith Difference at Lent."

12. See the discussion of cheap vs. costly grace in Bonhoeffer, *The Cost of Discipleship*, 43–56.

means cheap. We cheapen our costly salvation and priceless Jesus when the quality of our faith is not costly.

A seminary student of mine, Calin Popa, who was born and raised in Romania, told me that "Salvation is free" is a claim that Western Christians brought to Romania after the fall of communism and the doors to the West were opened. Before the doors were opened, the message among Romanian churches was more like "Salvation will cost you dearly. You can go to jail for free." Pastors who warned their congregants of the costliness of the faith knew that their next sermon could be their last message to their congregation. One never knew if the authorities would come and take them away to prison. Calin went on to say,

> During communism Christians lived under the threat of humiliation, intimidation, joblessness, beatings, torture, interrogation, jail, forced labor, and execution. There was little emphasis on salvation being "free" because there was no way to hide the cost. And although it was hard and many compromised under pressure betraying their brothers, the church as a whole was used to paying a high price for following Christ. After Romania opened to the West, the gospel came in as "free," and people started looking at it as free fire insurance more than as a costly relationship. The cost was not extracted from them by the communists anymore, and for a while they thought that there was no cost. Yet the cost was and is high because today the children and grandchildren of those who resisted persecution are seduced by the false consumerist gospel message of salvation without a cost to self.

The challenge that we all face in the West and elsewhere is the need to guard against using the faith for personal gain and profit. It is almost as if we are playing spiritual monopoly. In Monopoly, one dreads the Community Chest card, "Go to jail—go directly to jail—Do not pass Go, do not collect $200." Much better is the card "Get out of jail, free." You can keep it until you need it. If only the spiritual life with all its consequences for our actions were that easy! I wonder how often those of us in the West look at our faith as if it is nothing more than spiritual monopoly.

Spiritual monopoly isn't really a game, though. One can really lose one's soul, if one takes the "Get out of jail, free" card to represent a materialistic and consumeristic view of the gospel, which supposedly allows for an easy way out of one's troubles and conflicts. Certainly, God's grace is free, but it will cost us our lives in various ways to follow Christ. May God not allow us to leverage the faith to profit ourselves. May God leverage our lives to profit *the* faith. For Jesus said, "For what will it profit a man if he gains the whole world and forfeits his soul? Or what shall a man give in return for his soul?" (Matt 16:26). "Blessed are those who are persecuted for righteousness' sake, for theirs is the kingdom of heaven" (Matt 5:10).

Cultural Reflection: Is Suffering for the Christian Faith Salt in the Wounds?

I admire my friend Abir greatly. She is one of the strongest Christians I know, and is a person full of wisdom and discernment. But such strength and wisdom come with a price tag of suffering. Abir is an American citizen, who is of Palestinian descent. Her father is a Muslim, who struggled when she became a Christian given Christianity's associations in his mind with Western political powers that he believes often disregard and dehumanize Arabs and Muslims. Abir's evangelical American Christian brothers and sisters struggle with making space in their hearts for Palestinians, including Christians, not unlike Israel's security guards when she passes through checkpoints back in Palestine. Where does she turn? To Jesus. Not to the "Jesus" associated with a Christian Zionism in the States that discounts Palestinian concerns on the West Bank and Gaza Strip, but to Jesus, the Palestinian Jew from Nazareth, her fellow Semite. After all, Palestinian Christians trace their history back to the founding of the church in Palestine.

Like David in Uganda (discussed in the prior cultural reflection), Abir is a person of peace and a peacemaker (Matt 5:9). She longs for a just and equitable peace for Israel and the Palestinians. She also longs for American Christians to make peace with our faith and return to the Jesus of the New Testament. All too often, we are committed to preserving religious liberties here in the States. Now, religious liberty is not a bad thing. One could even say it's a very good thing unless it stands in the way of being slaves to Jesus and his righteous kingdom. All too often, we want to avoid persecution and will do nearly anything to preserve our liberties, failing to account for how Jesus said we are to be the salt of the earth—a preserving influence that is willing to suffer for the sake of making equitable peace in our society and the world. As noted in the biblical reflection on this passage, our saltiness as Jesus' disciples is lost when we seek to avoid suffering and religious persecution and so won't make peace (connect Matt 5:9 and 10 with 5:11–13). To repeat a point in that biblical reflection, Old Testament sacrifices were salted. Salt loses its import biblically when we don't bear witness to Jesus as living sacrifices who endure suffering and persecution for his righteous name's sake (Matt 5:10–13; see also Lev 2:13; Ezek 43:24; Ezra 6:9).

We Christians need to account for our ancient faith rather than seek to avoid persecution and tribulation, which includes longing and praying for Jesus to take us out of this world. Contrary to what many Christians think, it is my firm conviction that Jesus never promises to take us out of tribulation, but to keep and preserve us in the midst of it (John 17:15; Rev 3:10).[13] Just as the kingdom is present and future, so our hope is not a hope jettisoned to some remote heavenly state, but one in which Jesus' future kingdom breaks into our present suffering condition. As Matthew 5:10 reminds us, we are blessed for being persecuted by identifying with the Palestinian Jewish Jesus of the Bible. The kingdom of heaven belongs to us now!

Some American Christians might think they're being persecuted for their faith when they get pushback for making disparaging remarks about Muslims or Arabs. In contrast, Abir has received pushback for trying to reconcile her Christian and Palestinian identity. She is viewed with suspicion for cherishing Arab Muslims as fellow humans, too. Moreover, Abir agonizes how American

---

13. Gundry, *The Church and the Tribulation*, 58.

evangelicals easily place national allegiance and security concerns over security and solidarity in Jesus as the church globally. Their faulty priorities lead them to treat their brothers and sisters in Jesus in Arab lands as expendable for America's war on terror. But will this war as it is waged now only increase the threat of terror as it increases divisions between the Arab world and the West? How will we bridge the gap, as the Palestinian and Arab Christians who have often served as our only links and as agents of shalom in the region, experience increased risk of death and forced exile because of retaliation at the feet of Christian American missteps?[14]

No doubt, Abir has shed some salty tears, but no matter how hard it is, the struggle's worth it. She realizes that her suffering for the faith is not ultimately salt in her wounds. Her sufferings in Jesus here and abroad are bound up with being salt of the earth. Better salty tears than salt without sacrifice. The former is priceless. The latter has no value: "You are the salt of the earth, but if salt has lost its taste, how shall its saltiness be restored? It is no longer good for anything except to be thrown out and trampled under people's feet" (Matt 5:13).

Abir stands in a long line of Jesus' disciples going back to first-century Palestine, and to the prophets of old who came before them. These people of faith chose allegiance to Jesus over all other associations: "Blessed are you when others revile you and persecute you and utter all kinds of evil against you falsely on my account. Rejoice and be glad, for your reward is great in heaven, for so they persecuted the prophets who were before you" (Matt 5:11–12).

A prophetic, reconciling life has value now and in the future, unlike a pathetic life that seeks after material reward. Such materialistic aims include numerical church growth resulting from catering to people's consumerist and nationalistic preferences here and abroad. The kingdom of mammon has already come, but unlike Jesus' kingdom, it won't last forever.

14. Belt, "Arab Christians," 8.

Questions

1. As with the beatitude on mourning (Matt 5:4), why is it that being persecuted involves being blessed (Matt 5:10)?

2. How do you discern if you are being persecuted, when you experience pushback for your faith in Jesus? Is persecution the same thing as the loss of Christian privilege? Why or why not?

3. How does peacemaking (Matt 5:9) and being persecuted in this context (Matt 5:10) relate to one another?

4. What can be done for you to become and remain a salty Christian in view of Matthew 5:13?

5. Many American Christians live sheltered lives—we experience incredible religious freedom and tolerance. What might Abir's story teach us about how we in the West can become more sympathetic and sensitive to the plight of Christians from around the world who are experiencing dramatic persecution? How might their influence reframe our awareness of the Christian faith? How might their experience lead us to approach suffering as believers in Jesus?

6. As with Matthew 5:3, which indicates that those who are poor in spirit are already blessed, why are those who are persecuted for righteousness sake also blessed (see also Matt 5:10)? What is the significance of their being blessed in the present state rather than the blessing being completely future?

7. What would/will keep you going as a Christian in the face of persecution? What bearing might connection to Jesus, connection to the prophets of old, connection to our believing peers, and the kingdom of heaven have on this question (Matt 5:10–12)?

Conclusion

Don't Forget to Bring Your Bag Full of Blessings and Curses to the Promised Land

You may recall Irving Berlin's song, "God Bless America" (©1938/1939). The song or hymn of praise to and for America opens with concern over storm clouds gathering overseas, perhaps an allusion to the growing international conflict that would become World War I. The song is viewed as a "solemn prayer" that beseeches God to protect and guide America (including her mountains, prairies, and oceans) with a light from above through the night.

Apart from Reverend Jeremiah Wright's famous or infamous sermon chastising America with the line "God Damn America,"[1] I rarely find sermons or songs with titles like "God Curse America." For all the biblical allusions in America's history involving Manifest Destiny and that America is the New Israel, I seldom find that our country's principal voices and seers draw analogies to Israel when it comes to God's cursing his people. Even Israel and Judah had difficulty with such prophetic rebukes, as in the case of Jeremiah and the opposition by the false prophets to his prophetic denunciations.

---

1. Wright delivered his sermon entitled, "Confusing God and Government," at Trinity United Church of Christ on April 13, 2003. The full transcript can be found here: http://www.blackpast.org/2008-rev-jeremiah -wright-confusing-god-and-government.

Jeremiah was in good company. Moses instructed the people of Israel to recite upon entrance to the promised land the blessings for holding firmly to God's law and the curses for failing to obey the law (Deut 27–28). Moreover, the Lord Jesus himself does not simply bless or honor those who reflect his kingdom values, as set forth in the Beatitudes of Matthew 5. He also curses or shames the religious establishment in his day, as set forth in Matthew 23.

As discussed throughout this book, the Beatitudes (often rendered blessings) in Matthew 5 reflect what Jesus esteems, including spiritual humility, a passion for righteousness and purity of heart, and the pursuit of just peace. The curses in Matthew 23 have been taken to parallel the Beatitudes in Matthew 5 and serve as bookends to Jesus' public teaching ministry. In this way, together, they run parallel to the blessings and curses recorded in the Sermon on the Plain in Luke's Gospel (Luke 6:20–26). Moreover, they are reminiscent of Israel's recitation of the blessings and curses on the way to the promised land (Deut 27–28).[2]

I do not ultimately apply this biblical imagery involving Israel to America, though many have. I believe Jesus' words in the Sermon on the Mount are directed primarily to his disciples, and not the nation of Israel. Thus, I believe his words have primary import for the church. Not everyone agrees. For example, some maintain that a future state of Israel is Jesus' primary focus. Others maintain that he is addressing Israel as a nation in his own day. Perhaps there are other interpretive options. In any event, his words do have bearing on the life of the church.

We always think of Jesus loving and blessing people, like little children, and as he blesses and honors his disciples in the Beatitudes. But do we ever stop to wonder what he despised? Jesus despised and denounced spiritual pride, hypocrisy, and unjust

---

2. See N. T. Wright's discussion of the Beatitudes and curses in Matthew 5 and 23 respectively and his linking of them to the blessings and curses in Deuteronomy 27 and 28 in *The New Testament and the People of God*, 386–88. See also the comparisons and contrasts of the blessings and curses in Matthew 5 and Matthew 23 in K. C. Hanson's article, "How Honorable! How Shameful!" 101–4.

practices. We see such denunciations on display in the seven woes of Matthew 23. I have set forth excerpts of the seven woes here:

> But woe to you, scribes and Pharisees, hypocrites! For you shut the kingdom of heaven in people's faces. For you neither enter yourselves nor allow those who would enter to go in. (Matt 23:13–14)

> Woe to you, scribes and Pharisees, hypocrites! For you travel across sea and land to make a single proselyte, and when he becomes a proselyte, you make him twice as much a child of hell as yourselves. (Matt 23:15)

> Woe to you, blind guides, who say, "If anyone swears by the temple, it is nothing, but if anyone swears by the gold of the temple, he is bound by his oath." (Matt 23:16)

> Woe to you, scribes and Pharisees, hypocrites! For you tithe mint and dill and cumin, and have neglected the weightier matters of the law: justice and mercy and faithfulness. (Matt 23:23)

> Woe to you, scribes and Pharisees, hypocrites! For you clean the outside of the cup and the plate, but inside they are full of greed and self-indulgence. (Matt 23:25)

> Woe to you, scribes and Pharisees, hypocrites! For you are like whitewashed tombs, which outwardly appear beautiful, but within are full of dead people's bones and all uncleanness. So you also outwardly appear righteous to others, but within you are full of hypocrisy and lawlessness. (Matt 23:27–28)

> Woe to you, scribes and Pharisees, hypocrites! For you build the tombs of the prophets and decorate the monuments of the righteous, saying, "If we had lived in the days of our fathers, we would not have taken part with them in shedding the blood of the prophets." Thus you witness against yourselves that you are sons of those who murdered the prophets. (Matt 23:29–31)

What are we to make of these woes or curses? Beware of spiritual pride, hypocrisy, and unjust practices. Be attentive to what Jesus esteems, as recorded in Matthew's account of the Beatitudes that were offered as part of his sermon on the mount/mountain.

Still, it is easy when one has been on the mountain looking over the promised land to forget that there will be days in the valley below. It is also easy during good times to let down one's guard and forget to remain vigilant. So, it might help us from time to time to reenact the blessings as well as the curses. After all, Moses instructed the people of Israel to have some of the tribes recite the blessings on Mount Gerizim and other tribes to recite the curses on Mount Ebal upon crossing the Jordan River into the promised land (Deut 27:11–13).

In this light, I recommend at the close of this book to have those studying the Beatitudes together to break up into two groups: one group to recite Matthew 5:1–12 and the other group to recite Matthew 23:13–36. A word to the wise. Don't think that if you are the side offering the curse that your side gets a free pass and that only the other side is the intended referent! After all, as the Lord Jesus says just prior to the first woe: those who exalt themselves will be humbled and those who humble themselves will be exalted (Matt 23:12)! Besides, the very first beatitude signifies that all of Jesus' disciples are to be poor in spirit! In any event, the twelve tribes of Israel were beneficiaries of the blessings and curses as it played out in history. Another word to the wise: today's disciple, if not careful, may become tomorrow's Pharisee, or that generation of Israel that eventually experiences exile.

As noted earlier, the blessings and curses bookend Jesus' public teachings in Matthew's Gospel. Thus, they function to provide for us the beginning and end of his delivering of the messianic law. There is more, though. At the close of the Torah, Moses looks forward to Jesus' coming. Jesus fulfills Moses' promise to the people that God would stand beside Israel and guide her, delivering her by Joshua (Deut 31:1–6). Jesus is the Greek rendition of the Hebrew for Joshua, which signifies salvation or deliverance. Jesus is also God in their midst—Immanuel (Matt 1:23). Moses closes the Torah with this promise. Even though Israel will forsake God,

God will never forsake Israel, or the church made up of Jews and gentiles, given his promises to the patriarchs and through Jesus. Blessings and curses aside, God's ultimate promise to be with us will never falter or fail. God in Jesus will be with us always the whole of every day until the end of the age.[3]

> So Moses continued to speak these words to all Israel. And he said to them, "I am 120 years old today. I am no longer able to go out and come in. The LORD has said to me, 'You shall not go over this Jordan.' The LORD your God himself will go over before you. He will destroy these nations before you, so that you shall dispossess them, and Joshua will go over at your head, as the LORD has spoken. And the LORD will do to them as he did to Sihon and Og, the kings of the Amorites, and to their land, when he destroyed them. And the LORD will give them over to you, and you shall do to them according to the whole commandment that I have commanded you. Be strong and courageous. Do not fear or be in dread of them, for it is the Lord your God who goes with you. He will not leave you or forsake you." (Deut 31:1–6)

While Moses died and did not enter the blessed rest in the promised land with Israel, he will enter it along with all God's people through Jesus, as Hebrews indicates (Heb 11:39–40). Moreover, while Jesus died, he rose again and leads his people forward to the promised land or kingdom of heaven envisioned in the Beatitudes and Sermon on the Mount, which will be embodied in his community on behalf of all the nations.[4]

In this light, after reading out loud the blessings and curses of Matthew 5 and 23, I encourage the same readers to recite Deuteronomy 31:1–6 (quoted above) and Matthew 28:18–20, which reads:

> And Jesus came and said to them, "All authority in heaven and on earth has been given to me. Go therefore

3. Refer back to D. A. Carson's discussion of the literal language of Matthew 28:20 referenced in the introduction: *God with Us,* 163.

4. Refer to Wright's treatment of the biblical metanarrative involving Moses and Jesus in *The New Testament and the People of God,* 388–89.

and make disciples of all nations, baptizing them in the name of the Father and of the Son and of the Holy Spirit, teaching them to observe all that I have commanded you. And behold, I am with you always, to the end of the age." (Matt 28:18–20)

More than a great commission, we find here God's ultimate blessing and honorable affirmation in Jesus through the Spirit. The ultimate beatitude results from God's faithfulness in the face of our wavering and fickle faith on the way to and within the promised land. This blessing and honor is the great communion—God with us, Immanuel.

Bibliography

Augustine. *The Confession of St. Augustine*. Translated by Rex Warner. New York: Mentor, 1963.

———. *Of the Morals of the Catholic Church*. Translated by Richard Stothert. Vol. 4 of *The Nicene and Post-Nicene Fathers*, Series 1. Edited by Philip Schaff; 1886–89. 14 vols. Buffalo, NY: Christian Literature, 1887. Revised and edited for New Advent by Kevin Knight. Accessed August 5, 2017. http://www.newadvent.org/fathers/1401.htm.

Bailey, Kenneth. *Jesus through Middle Eastern Eyes: Cultural Studies in the Gospels*. Downers Grove, IL: IVP, 2008.

Bailey, Sarah Pulliam. "'God Has Given Trump Authority to Take Out Kim Jong Un,' Evangelical Adviser Says." *The Washington Post*, August 8, 2017. Accessed August 9, 2017. http://www.msn.com/en-us/news/us/%e2%80%98god-has-given-trump-authority-to-take-out-kim-jong-un%e2%80%99-evangelical-adviser-says/ar-AApK3qN.

Barnes, Albert. *Notes on the New Testament*. Edited by Robert Frew. Vol. 9 in *Barnes' Notes*. 1884–85. Reprint, Grand Rapids: Baker, 1985.

Barth, Karl. *Church Dogmatics*, IV/2: *The Doctrine of Reconciliation*. Edited by G. W. Bromiley and T. F. Torrance. Edinburgh: T. & T. Clark, 1958.

BBC. "Islamic State: Egyptian Christians Held in Libya 'Killed.'" February 15th, 2015. Accessed on July 29, 2017. http://www.bbc.com/news/world-31481797.

Belt, Don. "Arab Christians: The Forgotten Faithful." *National Geographic*, June 2009. Accessed August 10, 2017. http://ngm.nationalgeographic.com/2009/06/arab-christians/belt-text.

Blomberg, Craig L. *Jesus and the Gospels: An Introduction and Survey*. 2nd ed. Nashville: Broadman and Holman, 2009.

Bonhoeffer, Dietrich. *The Cost of Discipleship*. 1959. Reprint. New York: Touchstone, 1995.

———. *Letters and Papers from Prison*. Edited by Eberhard Bethge. Enlarged ed. New York: Touchstone, 1997.

Bruce, Alexander. *The Expositor's Greek Testament*. Edited by W. Robertson Nicoll. Vol. 1. Grand Rapids: Eerdmans, 1930.

Bibliography

Bruner, Frederick Dale. *Matthew: A Commentary. Vol 1: The Christbook, Matthew 1–12*. Rev. and exp. ed. Grand Rapids: Eerdmans, 2004.

Calvin, John. *A Harmony of the Gospels: Matthew, Mark and Luke*. Vol. 1 in Calvin's Commentaries. Translated by A. W. Morrison. Edited by David W. Torrance and Thomas F. Torrance. Grand Rapids: Eerdmans, 1972.

Carson, Clayborne, ed. *The Autobiography of Martin Luther King, Jr*. New York: Warner, 1998.

Carson, D. A. *God with Us: Themes from Matthew*. Reprint. Eugene, OR: Wipf & Stock, 1995.

———. *Matthew*. Vol. 8 of *Expositor's Bible Commentary*. Edited by Frank E. Gaebelein, 1–599. Grand Rapids: Zondervan, 1984.

———. *The Sermon the Mount: An Evangelical Exposition of Matthew 5–7*. Grand Rapids: Baker, 1982.

Chesterton, G. K. *What's Wrong with the World*. Reprint. San Francisco: Ignatius, 1994.

Chui, Angie. "21 Christians Slain to be Declared Martyrs by the Coptic Church." *Christianity Today*, March 1st, 2015. Accessed on July 29, 2017. https://www.christiantoday.com/article/21.christians.slain.by.isis.to.be.declared.martyrs.by.coptic.church/48657.htm.

CNN. "ISIS Message to Christians: 'We're Coming to Get You." February 15, 2017. Accessed on July 29, 2017. http://www.cnn.com/videos/tv/2015/02/17/cnn-tonight-don-lemon-isis-reese-francona-terror-threat-libya-isis-weiss.cnn

Daily Mail. "Scientists Discover that Eyes Really are 'the Window to the Soul,'" February 19, 2007. Accessed on July 28, 2017. http://www.dailymail.co.uk/sciencetech/article-436932/Scientists-discover-eyes-really-window-soul.html#ixzz3RufUmpsP.

Davies, W. D., and Dale C. Allison, Jr. *A Critical and Exegetical Commentary on the Gospel according to Saint Matthew*. International Critical Commentary. 1988. Reprint. London: T. & T. Clark, 2004.

———. *The Setting of the Sermon on the Mount*. Cambridge: Cambridge University Press, 1964.

Deddo, Cathy. "Sermon on the Mount Bible Study: Chapter 5:5–6." Accessed on July 28, 2017. http://www.trinitystudycenter.com/mount/matthew_5-5-6.php.

Ellicott, C. J. *Ellicott's Bible Commentary in One Volume*. 1971. Reprint. Grand Rapids: Zondervan, 1976.

France, R. T. *The Gospel of Matthew*. The New International Commentary on the New Testament. Grand Rapids: Eerdmans, 2007.

Greenman, Jeffrey P., Timothy Larsen, and Stephen R. Spencer, eds. *The Sermon on the Mount through the Centuries: From the Early Church to John Paul II*. Grand Rapids: Brazos, 2007.

Gundry, Robert H. *The Church and the Tribulation: A Biblical Examination of Posttribulationism*. Grand Rapids: Zondervan, 1973.

————. *Commentary on the New Testament: Verse-by-Verse Explanations with Literal Translations*. Peabody, MA: Hendrickson, 2010.

————. *Matthew: A Commentary on His Literary and Theological Art*. Grand Rapids: Eerdmans, 1982.

Hagner, Donald. *Matthew 1–13*. Word Biblical Commentary 33A. Nashville: Thomas Nelson, 2000.

Hanson, K. C. "How Honorable! How Shameful! A Cultural Analysis of Matthew's Makarisms and Reproaches." *Semeia* 68 (1996) 81–104.

Hare, Douglas R. A. *Matthew*. Interpretation. Louisville, KY: Westminster John Knox, 1993.

Harmon, Daniel E. *Central and East Africa: 1880 to the Present: From Colonialism to Civil War*. Philadelphia: Chelsea House, 2002.

Hendriksen, William. *The Exposition of the Gospel According to Matthew*. New Testament Commentary. Grand Rapids: Baker, 1982.

Hirsch, Emil G., and Thomas Kelly Cheyne, Isidore Singer, and Isaac Brodyé. "Isaiah." In *The Jewish Encyclopedia*. Accessed on August 24, 2017. http://www.jewishencyclopedia.com/articles/8235-isaiah.

Jackson, Wayne. "Matthew 5:5—Meek Inherit the Earth." Accessed on July 28, 2017. https://www.christiancourier.com/articles/905-matthew-5-5-meek-inherit-the-earth.

Kalas, J. Ellsworth. *Beatitudes from the Back Side: A Different Take on What It Means to be Blessed*. Nashville: Abingdon, 2008.

Keener, Craig S. *The Gospel of Matthew: A Socio-Rhetorical Commentary*. Grand Rapids: Eerdmans, 2009.

King Jr., Martin Luther. *A Testament of Hope: The Essential Writings and Speeches of Martin Luther King, Jr.*, edited by James M. Washington, 253–58. San Francisco: HarperCollins, 1991.

————. "Loving Your Enemies." Accessed on August 11, 2017. http://kingencyclopedia.stanford.edu/encyclopedia/documentsentry/doc_loving_your_enemies.

Kohler, Kaufmann. "Zealots." In *The Jewish Encyclopedia*. Accessed on August 24, 2017. http://www.jewishencyclopedia.com/articles/15185-zealots.

Kuruvilla, Carol. "Coptic Christian Bishop Angaelos Forgives ISIS for Libya Massacre." *Huffington Post,* February 21, 2015. Accessed on July 29, 2017. http://www.huffingtonpost.com/2015/02/21/bishop-angaelos-forgives-isis_n_6725726.html.

Kutz, Karl. "Torah Scroll Dedication." Speech given at Multnomah University, February 5, 2015.

Kweifio-Okai, Carla. "Papua New Guinea Has World's Worst Access to Clean Water, Says Water Aid." *The Guardian*, March 21, 2016. Accessed February 14, 2017. https://www.theguardian.com/global-development/2016/mar/22/papua-new-guinea-worst-access-clean-water-wateraid.

Ladd, George Eldon. *The Gospel of the Kingdom: Scriptural Studies in the Kingdom of God*. 1959. Reprint. Grand Rapids: Eerdmans, 1988.

Bibliography

Lapide, Pinchas. *The Sermon on the Mount: Utopia or Program for Action?* Translated by Arlene Swidler. Rev. ed. Maryknoll, NY: Orbis, 1986.

Macrae, Fiona. "Junk Food Alters Brain Chemistry and Leads to Bingeing." *Daily Mail*, September 16, 2009. Accessed July 28, 2017. http://www.dailymail. co.uk/health/article-1213753/Junk-food-alters-brain-chemistry-leads-bingeing.html.

Marrus, Michael R., ed. *The Nazi Holocaust, Part 8: Bystanders to the Holocaust.* Vol. 3 of *The Nazi Holocaust: Historical Articles on the Destruction of the European Jews.* 1989. Reprint. Boston: De Gruyter Saur, 2011.

McKnight, Scot. *The King Jesus Gospel: The Original Good News Revisited.* Grand Rapids: Zondervan 2011.

———. *Sermon on the Mount.* The Story of God Bible Commentary. Grand Rapids: Zondervan, 2013.

———. "The Sermon on the Mount as Gospel." *Jesus Creed Patheos*, November 18, 2013. http://www.patheos.com/blogs/jesuscreed/2013/11/18/the-sermon-on-the-mount-as-gospel/#jriMMiiMIK5LkMjK.99.

Metzger, Paul Louis. "What Is Biblical Justice?" *Leadership* 31.3 (2010) 25.

Minear, Paul. "The Salt of the Earth." *Interpretation* 51 (1997) 31–41.

Moltmann, Jürgen. *The Crucified God: The Cross of Christ as the Foundation and Criticism of Christian Theology.* Minneapolis: Fortress, 1993.

———. *God for a Secular Society: The Public Relevance of Theology.* Minneapolis: Fortress, 1999.

Newman, Alex. "Christian Martyrdom Doubled in 2013, Persecution Growing." *The New American*, January 16, 2014. Accessed on July 29, 2017 https:// www.thenewamerican.com/culture/faith-and-morals/item/17417-christian-martyrdom-doubled-in-2013-persecution-growing.

Oakesmith, John. *The Religion of Plutarch: A Pagan Creed of Apostolic Times.* New York: Longmans, Green, & Co., 1902.

O'Connor, April. "Fourth Time's a Charm: How Donald Trump Made Bankruptcy Work for Him." *Forbes*, April 29, 2011. Accessed on August 4, 2017. https://www.forbes.com/sites/clareoconnor/2011/04/29/fourth-times-a-charm-how-donald-trump-made-bankruptcy-work-for-him.

Pritchett, V. S. Endorsement of *Les Misérables* by Victor Hugo. Translated by Charles E. Wilbour. New York: Modern Library, 1992.

Psychology Today. "Emotional Intelligence." Accessed on August 5, 2017. https://www.psychologytoday.com/basics/emotional-intelligence.

Rashad, Jonathan. "Coptic Christian Village Mourns ISIS Victims in Libya." *Newsweek,* March 8, 2015. Accessed on http://www.newsweek.com/ photos-coptic-christian-village-mourns-isis-killings-libya-311198.

Stewart, Tim. "God Comforts the Afflicted and Afflicts the Comfortable." Accessed on July 28, 2017. http://www.dictionaryofchristianese.com/god-comforts-the-afflicted-and-afflicts-the-comfortable.

Stott, John R. W. *The Message of the Sermon on the Mount: Matthew 5–7: Christian Counter-Culture.* The Bible Speaks Today. Downers Grove, IL: IVP, 1978.

Bibliography

Woodley, Matt. *The Gospel of Matthew: God with Us*. Resonate Series. Downers Grove, IL: IVP, 2011.

World Health Organization. "Key Facts from JMP 2015 Report." Accessed January 22, 2017. http://www.who.int/water_sanitation_health/monitoring/jmp-2015-key-facts/en.

Wright, N. T. *The Challenge of Jesus: Rediscovering Who Jesus Was and Is*. Downers Grove, IL: IVP, 2015.

———. *Matthew for Everyone, Part I: Chapters 1–15*. The New Testament Is for Everyone. 2nd ed. Louisville, KY: Westminster John Knox, 2004.

———. *The New Testament and the People of God*. Vol. 1 in Christian Origins and the Question of God. London: SPCK, 1992.

———. "Righteousness." In *The New Dictionary of Theology*, edited by David F. Wright, Sinclair B. Ferguson, and J. I. Packer, 590–92. Leicester, UK: IVP, 1988.

Index

Index